TOUGH CHOICES

TOUGH CHOICES

STRUCTURED PATERNALISM AND

THE LANDSCAPE OF CHOICE

SIGAL R. BEN-PORATH

PRINCETON UNIVERSITY PRESS

PRINCETON AND OXFORD

In the United Kingdom: Princeton University Press, 6 Oxford Street,
Woodstock, Oxfordshire OX20 1TW

Library of Congress Cataloging-in-Publication Data

Ben-Porath, Sigal R., 1967–
Tough choices : structured paternalism and the landscape of choice /
Sigal R. Ben-Porath.
p. cm.
Includes bibliographical references and index.
ISBN 978-0-691-14641-6 (hardcover : alk. paper)
1. Democracy—Philosophy.   2. Paternalism—Political aspects.
3. Civil rights.   4. Social values.   5. Politics and culture.
6. Freedom of expression.   I. Title.
JC423.B3437 2010
320.01'9—dc22   2009044077

British Library Cataloging-in-Publication Data is available

This book has been composed in Minion

Printed on acid-free paper. ∞

press.princeton.edu

Printed in the United States of America

1 3 5 7 9 10 8 6 4 2

To Eran Noah, Itamar Eldad, and Amalia Ruth

CONTENTS

—m—

ACKNOWLEDGMENTS

—ᶜᵐ—

MANY COLLEAGUES AND FRIENDS contributed to the process of writing this book, first at Princeton University's Center for Human Values and later at the University of Pennsylvania. For comments on anything from preliminary ideas to previous drafts of the book, I am thankful to Anita Allen, Danielle Allen, Bat-Ami Bar-On, Eran Ben-Porath, Harry Brighouse, Eamonn Callan, Orna Coussin, Suzanne Dovi, James Dwyer, Marilyn Friedman, Joan Goodman, Amy Gutmann, Michael Hand, David Hansen, Michael Katz, J. Donald Moon, Marlisa Morchella, Rob Reich, Hollis Robbins, Tamar Schapiro, William Scheuerman, Marion Smiley, Rogers Smith, Jeff Spinner-Halev, Mariah Zeisberg, and two anonymous reviewers for Princeton University Press.

I am grateful to Ian Malcolm for his steadfast support, for the books he provided, and for his good humor. Phillip Buckley and Christopher Pupik Dean provided excellent research assistance. Writing was generously supported by the Spencer Foundation.

Parts of this book were presented at Princeton University's Center for Human Values; the American Political Science Association; the Midwest Political Science Association; the 2007 Villemain Annual Lecture on Education, Democracy, and the Public Life at San Jose University; Tel-Aviv University; the SPEL Forum at SUNY–Binghamton; the Philosophy of Education forum at Teachers College, and the Dewey Seminar on Education, Democracy and Justice at the Institute for Advanced Studies in Princeton. I thank the organizers, the commentators, and the audiences in all these forums.

ACKNOWLEDGMENTS

Part of chapter 3 appeared in *Constellations* in an article titled "On Government Regulation of Intimate Life"; part of chapter 4 appeared in the *Journal of Philosophy of Education* in an article titled "Autonomy and Vulnerability"; an earlier version of chapter 6 appeared in the *Journal of Philosophy of Education*. I thank these publications for permission to use these materials.

We do not get to choose most of our family members, but I cannot imagine doing any better had I had the chance to choose each one of mine. This book is dedicated to Eran Noah, whom I choose again every day, and to my beloved Itamar and Amalia, who like all children are the result of a complex set of lotteries, and are thus a living proof for me that choice can be much overrated.

—ᴡ— 1 —ᴡ—

To Choose or Not to Choose?

Choice in Social and Political Thought

For most of Western political history, a majority of individuals had little opportunity to make choices about critical aspects of their lives. Social structure was formal and rigid; one was born into a given social status, with a clear life plan and very limited opportunity to alter its course. Being a good member of one's family, class, gender, and profession involved abiding by strict rules, following a course set by ancestors, social norms, and other dimensions of destiny. Think of Oliver Twist's start in life in Charles Dickens's description:

> What an excellent example of the power of dress, young Oliver Twist was! Wrapped in the blanket which had hitherto formed his only covering, he might have been the child of a nobleman or a beggar; it would have been hard for the haughtiest stranger to have assigned him his proper station in society. But now that he was enveloped in the old calico robes which had grown yellow in the same service, he was badged and ticketed, and fell into his place at once—a parish child—the orphan of a workhouse—the humble, half-starved drudge—to be cuffed and buffeted through the world—despised by all, and pitied by none. (p. 4)

Oliver's prospects for the future become even more apparent when we compare him to the station of Mr. Fitzwilliam Darcy, an-

1

other fictional young man (though not an infant) living outside of London in the early nineteenth century. Here is his first appearance in Jane Austen's *Pride and Prejudice*:

> Mr. Darcy soon drew the attention of the room by his fine, tall person, handsome features, noble mien; and the report which was in general circulation within five minutes after his entrance, of his having ten thousand a year. The gentlemen pronounced him to be a fine figure of a man, the ladies declared he was much handsomer than Mr. Bingley, and he was looked at with great admiration for about half the evening, till his manners gave a disgust which turned the tide of his popularity; for he was discovered to be proud, to be above his company, and above being pleased; and not all his large estate in Derbyshire could then save him from having a most forbidding, disagreeable countenance. (p. 7)

In these times, as in many other times and places, an individual's life was largely determined by external circumstances. Of course, one could decide to be "agreeable" to a greater or lesser extent, inasmuch as such traits are within one's control. But these traits account for relatively minor variations within an allotted future. Among other things, one's place of residence, her health, her employment, and other conditions and decisions that create the contours of one's life were often strictly pre-charted before birth. Parental knowledge and social conventions were considered to be better directives than one's own judgment. Traditional groups and societies today impose similar limitations on personal choice, preferring social stability, continuity, and personal submission over self-expression, personal authenticity, ingenuity, and choice.

Strong arguments can be made for either sociopolitical system, and my intention here is not to compare them or to make the case for one over the other. Rather I take as my starting point the contemporary democratic, Western sociopolitical structure and ethos that favors choice over destiny. Freedom, exercised through the choice of a life plan, is the tool for overcoming the social vision of inherent inequality or structural stratification, such as the one evident from comparing Oliver Twist with Mr. Darcy. In contemporary democracies, social mobility is embraced as a manifestation of both liberty and equality. A person is not supposed to be confined to her birthplace and to a life plan sketched for her before birth. In addition to the endorsement of a diversity of aims, democratic discourse tends to assume (even if implicitly) a revisability of ends, accepting the possibility that individuals would at some point(s) in their lives rethink their affiliations, goals, values, and visions of the good life. The combination of value pluralism and the revisability of ends sets the foundation for a social structure in which significant space is provided for individual choice. In the American public sphere, and in much of Western philosophy and politics, the notion of choice serves as a panacea to a host of policy challenges, and as a conclusive response to the predetermined life such as that of the Victorian era or of traditional cultures. Choice offers equality of status, which stands in opposition to premodern and aristocratic visions of destined roles. Allowing individuals to develop a life plan, to chart their own paths, to be the authors of their lives, seems to offer an appropriate way to implement the values of equal standing and equal dignity.

But does choice as constructed in contemporary theory and policy truly provide such a comprehensive response? This book is an attempt to critically examine some of the ways in which choice is framed in contemporary theory and policy, and to suggest an alternative framework that balances choice and intervention in order to better achieve the twin goals of equality and freedom. The critical appraisal of choice developed here is to be understood as a constructive effort to enhance the social and political setting of choice, rather than as a traditionalist (or other) attempt to justify a social order that gives little room for choice. I look at the landscape of choice in search of ways to more fully achieve the promise of choice, namely, equal standing and freedom for all members of society regardless of their contingent, or morally arbitrary, characteristics and circumstances.

3

At first glance, choice does seem like an appropriate, straightforward solution to the shortcomings of the alternative, choice-less vision of the predestined life. The rationale for choice and its realization are enticingly simple and direct: the state should respect individuals by letting them develop and realize their preferences through making choices, thereby expressing and implementing equal dignity and opportunity. Their dignity as individuals and their equal status as citizens are expressed in their responsibility for their decisions and their consequences. The state should not limit choices; it should not intervene in the personal process of preference development and expression. It should keep its proverbial hands, or policies, out of the private business of pursuing what each individual sets as her goals, aspirations, and values.

But another look reveals that the state can grant various forms of freedom to choose, and it can frame and shape them in a variety of ways through social policies. The state's (or government's) decision to regulate or avoid regulating a particular realm—like marriage, for example, or mortgage lending—organizes that realm, providing individuals, groups, and institutions with a particular landscape in which to make their choices. Regulating marriage means that only certain people can marry (those who meet the criteria of that state at that time, possibly including race, age, and sexual identity) while keeping others outside that institution. The state can decide to avoid regulating the institution of marriage, and allow anyone to form relationships and families as they see fit. It can still forbid pedophilia, thus maintaining the age limitation on marriage, or it can ban homosexuality, thus maintaining the sexuality barrier to relationship. Any one of these actions by the state, including the deregulation or the decision to not regulate personal-social institutions like marriage, has significant consequences in shaping the landscape of options individuals face in this realm, thus shaping their identity, their preferences, and their actions. Similarly, in realms like banking or mortgage lending, the decision of whether and how the state regulates the conduct of private institutions affects the landscape of choices that both these institutions and the individuals they serve face. The ubiquity of sub-prime and insolvent mortgages is to a large extent the result of a decision to deregulate this field, or to lift previously existing regulations on mortgage lending institutions. The landscape of choice is thus significantly controlled by the state, through its legislative and regulatory systems, and its decisions, including decisions to not regulate or not to take action, form this landscape in which individuals and organizations make their choices.[1] The next questions to grapple with, thus, are: How is individual choice shaped by social policies? How do social policies limit or expand the landscape of individual choice, and how can such limitations and expansions be justified? To begin answering this question, which is at the heart of this book, I consider the role of choice in the liberal-democratic project.

The place of choice in contemporary political philosophy was etched by one of its most ardent proponents, John Stuart Mill. In *On Liberty*, Mill focuses on the view that liberty is of value as it facilitates individuality, which is to be understood centrally as self-creation, or as the opportunity to make one's own life. (Mill is also an advocate of the state's role in the flourishing and well-being of individuals, a point that he does not fully argue, and which will receive attention here.) Contemporary liberalism focuses on his harm principle, or the suggestion that one can make any choice about one's actions so long as others are not harmed by those choices and actions. The promise of this principle is that of self-authorship, the epitomized consequence of liberty and autonomy. Liberal democracies develop a host of policies on the basis of these values.

Implicit in the democratic ideal is the suggestion that citizens should be self-ruling both as a group and as individuals. This self-rule is often translated into, or equated with, an ability to choose. Respect for individuals is thus expressed by a refrain from intervention in the processes and outcomes of their choices. Decisions made through proper choosing processes are deemed justified and legitimate. Institutions that leave room for choice are perceived as

5

more desirable, a priori, than ones that direct individuals toward a specified outcome. In the American public debate, groups that favor making abortion available frame their position as "pro-choice"; school voucher supporters describe their position as allowing for "school choice"; attempts to reform health care falter time and again over the concern that reform would limit or eliminate individuals' opportunity to choose among health plans or doctors. The repeated reference to choice expresses an appeal to a shared value, echoing a valorization of the act of choosing. It reverberates in the public sphere in ways that intensify and further centralize the place of choice in the public consciousness. Hence, it is important to clarify the way this value functions in contemporary democracies, to sketch its advantages and limitations, or what it can do for us, and to examine ways in which it can better fulfill its promise.

Autonomy, Freedom, Opportunity

Most theoretical and empirical studies on choice focus on two related conditions for its implementation, namely, autonomy and freedom. The mainstream scholarly and political view on choice sees it as derivative of conditions of freedom and as based on the capabilities of individuals to autonomously express and execute their preferences.

A more elaborate account of the conditions of choice would suggest that for choice to be properly available in a democratic society, three types of conditions need to be satisfied. First, philosophically (and psychologically), autonomy needs to be developed and exercised. The basic properties of autonomy would include the development of an ability to discern and consider options, and the capability to act according to one's preferences. The second condition of choice is political: freedom must be part of the institutional ethos, allowing for the realization of rights, which in turn have to be engraved in the political structure. A third and less often considered condition for choice is the social one. Socially, opportunity must exist, or the availability of multiple relevant options for the individual to choose from (this third point is historically related to what T. H. Marshall terms "social rights"). To define opportunity in this context of choice-related policies, I consider X to have an opportunity to Y if Y is part of a choice set that is available and accessible to X.[2]

Absent one of these conditions— autonomy, freedom, and opportunity—choice is hampered, or becomes unavailable as a practice. These three aspects of choice are not independent, but neither can they be described as derivative of each other. For choice to be feasible and accessible, all three components need to be present, and moreover, they must augment each other. In other words, the fulfillment of all three conditions—autonomy, freedom, and opportunity—is necessary for the achievement of choice. The main challenge in conceptualizing the conditions for choice is the balance among the three, as well as the priorities set among them. Most liberal theorists suggest that ethical individualism, or the primacy of the individual over the group (including the state), justifies a prioritizing to autonomy as a manifestation of liberty and an expression of respect; in fact, many regard the legitimacy of the state to be conditioned upon the autonomy of its citizens. Counter to this widely held argument, I suggest that preferring opportunity, and prioritizing it (for the purpose of social policy making) over autonomy, can advance both equal respect to individuals and freedom. Autonomy in its minimal form is sufficiently available to individuals in democratic society; opportunity, on the other hand, is necessary for utilizing many forms of decision making that result from autonomous thinking. Consequently, facilitating opportunity can better implement both freedom and equality in a democratic society, and thus strengthen the legitimacy of the democratic state. As a result, civic equality should be understood as tied not only to autonomy and freedom but also to the conditions for well-being that are satisfied when appropriate opportunities are present in the individual's landscape of choice.

This book explores the impact of this restructured view of choice on policies, and the role that these policies in turn have on the landscape in which individuals make decisions and choices. In examining justifications for choice-related policies, the following chapters consider the merits of a change of focus from an emphasis on freedom and autonomy to an emphasis on the facilitation of opportunity as part of the conditions of civic equality. While freedom and autonomy are clearly valuable goals, prioritizing them when constructing a theory of choice that could serve as a framework for policy making can obscure some crucial aspects of choice, including those tied to identity, belonging, and affiliation. Prioritizing autonomy creates further risks, such as elitism and discrimination, if autonomy is understood as a condition for acquiring the policy's benefits. It can also undermine diversity by failing to appreciate those who do not espouse autonomy as a value. Logically speaking, autonomy is not a necessary condition for opportunity. While autonomy is commonly understood as a desirable personal trait or skill, opportunity is a condition offered through institutional structure and policy decisions. Such policies can assume the existence of autonomy or aspire to establish it, but they are not required to do either (and as I suggest later on, it is sometimes better if they do not). Therefore, the current discussion focuses on the expansion of opportunities that choice policies can provide when properly constructed, and considers autonomy as well as freedom either as background conditions for opportunities or as potential results, but not as preconditions or ultimate aims.

What difference does priority make in endorsing and expressing freedom, autonomy, and opportunity? The order of priority among these sometimes competing, sometimes complementing, values is expressed through policies that support the facilitation and protection of autonomy or the provision of opportunities according to perceived needs and specified circumstances. A policy that prioritizes autonomy would generally take one of two possible forms. First, it could be based on the assumption that individuals are already autonomous, and thus focus on nonintervention and liberty. Alternatively, it could express a perfectionist view that aspires to facilitate or develop autonomy in individuals. In this case, it would be more interventionist and would perceive of freedom as a positive value rather than as a state of nonintervention.

A policy that prioritizes opportunity would be based on a more robust responsibility of society toward the individual and on an active attempt to achieve civic equality, understood to include well-being. The suggestion that the state and society have an obligation to provide opportunities is an expansion of, rather than a substitution for, the state's obligation to support freedom and the facilitation of autonomy. Focusing on choice, with its normative and practical dimensions, requires greater emphasis on the state's responsibility to provide equal standing, choice sets, and opportunities to choose for all members.

These ideals are facilitated and pursued through the regulation of opportunities and choices, or, metaphorically, through cultivating a fruitful landscape of choice. At the center of the current investigation are policies and state-sanctioned regulations of choice; however, a fuller understanding of the conditions of choice would require an examination of the ways choices are made by individuals. Because many instances of choice boil down to the individual decision maker, the personal process of choosing merits a closer look. I therefore look beyond policy making and regulation, and consider cognitive, cultural, and intimate factors that affect the choices individuals make.

The two domains making up the landscape of choice—the political and the personal—converge in the realm of education, where individuals learn the skills and attitudes necessary for informed choice, and where policies that reflect society's priorities among the conditions of choice are negotiated and expressed. In the following chapters, I look at those instances of choice in which the tension between personal makeup and regulation is most significant; these cases seem to me to be most revealing when considering the proper balance between regulation and freedom, autonomy and equality, individuality and affiliation. Looking at decisions in which parenthood, culture, or religious belief are at stake can reveal the complex landscape of choice with its theoretical, personal, and policy dimensions. Moreover, these areas of choice require the most attention to individual differences. Individuals face choices in many other areas of their lives—which insurance policy to choose, for example, which car to buy, or which candidate or party to vote for. Some of these decisions will bear important consequences for their lives and the lives of others. However, decisions of this type do not require policy makers to devote as much attention to individual identities. They require less information about personal background, preferences, and connection. The tension between regulation and freedom in these cases is thus not as pronounced as in the cases of choosing how to educate one's children, or whether to leave an abusive relationship. These latter cases can thus tell us more about how personal desires and individual well-being are affected by social policies, and how social policies should be responsive to these personal differences, through being cognizant of their impact on the landscape of choice.

Motivation, Intervention, Regulation

Individual differences are most pronounced in circumstances of choice through variations in motivation. The reasons we have for choosing one option over another are broadly referred to as motivation, with the understanding that reasons can be influenced and shaped by external forces. The discussion of paternalism in the next chapter considers ways in which regulatory procedures, or forms of intervention, can shape individual preferences and thus motivation for action. Motivation is often not a proper target for regulatory policies, because directly affecting individuals' motivations could in many cases require a normative judgment by the state of the values they hold, their vision of the good life, and other dimensions of their personal, moral, or community-related identity. However, institutions and regulatory procedures can affect the level of participation in voluntary actions, without directly intervening in the internal life of the choosing individuals. For example, default rules—a form of regulatory policy—greatly affect participation in a host of programs, from savings to organ donation to attending neighborhood schools. Take the case of organ donation as an example. Recent studies show the effect of forms of registration on the level of participation, in comparing, on the one hand, states in which assumed consent is a default for all individuals (or all drivers), to states demanding expressed consent, or a conscious decision by individuals to register for the organ donation program.[3] While motivation to be a designated organ donor may not have changed as a result of the state instituting a new default rule according to which all drivers would be donors (unless they opt out), the actual participation of individuals in the organ donation program significantly increased as a result. Public campaigns and other educational interventions have a far less impressive effect on participation in comparable programs.

Note that if an individual holds a principled view on organ donation, her motivation will remain constant and so will her participation. For example, if she believes that it might harm her chances to go to heaven, or her reincarnation, or even if she is opposed to organ donation because of a sense of revulsion, she would opt out of the program. Others, who have a weaker motivation for or against organ donation, would opt for the default rule, whatever it may be. Thus, through instituting default rules, the state (or employer, or other regulator) can affect levels of participation in different programs, thus advancing what seems to be preferable—like organ donations—without imposing a change of motivation or preference on individuals, and without infringing upon their freedom.

The effects of default rules and other regulatory procedures on personal decisions provide us with a glimpse of the state's role in the construction of the landscape of choice. A careful consideration of these effects can provide some normative tools for assessing policies that affect this landscape. Considering what impact policies have on personal choices makes it possible to distinguish among various levels of motivation, and thus among various forms of justified and unjustified intervention. Consider the person who is adamantly opposed to organ donation for religious, aesthetic, or other reasons. Her freedom is maintained by the default rule of becoming an organ donor, as long as there is an opt-out option.[4] By instituting this rule, the state expresses a clear preference for organ donation, along with respect to those whose identities and views prohibit them from sharing this preference. Those whose motivations are weak and do not constitute a significant dimension of their (religious or other) identity are encouraged to share the preferred view (i.e., a positive vision on organ donation). Clearly, such regulated prioritizing of a preferred view requires some justification in itself. Mostly it will make sense in areas where properly deliberated expert opinion or strongly shared communal values can provide a solid basis for preferring one option—donating organs, saving for retirement—over others. These options too are context-based: in countries where the majority culture or religion opposes organ donation, or where the state provides for retirees through existing mechanisms, the preferred view on these matters may be different than in countries with no such shared values or existing mechanisms.

Even with this context-dependence caveat, some may be reluctant to trust "authorities," experts, or the state with such power. But it should be noted first that the state (and in other cases, other authorities—for example, employers or local government) already holds these powers. Moreover, failing to prioritize one option over others is often equivalent to actively mandating a preferred view, as the case of the mechanisms for designating organ donors makes clear. By not creating a default rule by which all drivers will be designated donors, the state does not step back and practice nonintervention. Rather, it endorses an opposition to organ donation by effectively instituting a default rule by which all drivers will not be organ donors unless they opt into the program. Therefore, the need to carefully design policies that generate, endorse, and implement a preferred view through creating an appropriate choice set, and, where appropriate, default rules and other mechanisms, does not expand the state's power. Rather, this approach simply requires the state to use its existing power more carefully and thoughtfully, and to spell out the values that its policy expresses.

The discussion of destructive intimate choices further complicates the picture. What should be made of choices that seem to be clearly bad for the individual who makes them, and sometimes destructive for others? How should these choices and acts be analyzed, and what would be a justified response to them, considering that these decisions can be closely aligned with the individual's deep sense of personal identity, self-worth, or moral vision? In the third chapter, I develop the view that while paternalism may be justified in regulating intimate choices, it should rarely take the form of criminalization. In other words, when the state is responding to destructive choices individuals make in the intimate sphere, intervention should be less blunt than the tools the criminal law and criminal justice system can offer. Using "softer" tools of regulation properly addresses the understanding of choices as tied to personal identity in ways that the state has little to contribute to (and sometimes little jurisdiction over). Intimate choices are at the borders of the landscape of choice, which is open to state regulation. Expressing this understanding by using appropriate regulatory tools would also prove more justified and productive as a public policy.

Throughout the book, the distinction between paternalism toward adults and that toward children is considered. Forming preferences and developing tools to reflect on them and express them is an essential part of the process of growing up. Choice-related policies should reflect this distinction between adults and children and address it directly. Adults too, however, often amend and revise their motivations and preferences, reconsider them, and look for new ways of expressing them. It is thus important to reflect on the ways in which adults and children differ, and the areas in which they should be regarded by the state similarly or distinctly.

13

In the various areas of policy that this book explores, it is mostly in search of a midway, perhaps a golden path, between unmitigated freedom and heavy regulation. In the realm of financial exchanges and the economy broadly, the search for a golden path draws the attention of economists and policy makers. In looking at policies beyond economics, the discussion here focuses on decision making in areas where personal identity is formed and expressed, and aims to implement similar visions of this golden path in areas of personal and social life as well.

A Note on Empirical Studies and Normative Theories

What should knowledge about the ways individuals choose tell us about policies that can best reflect respect for autonomy and rationality? Should liberal theory, with its strong emphasis on values such as freedom and respect, be altered to incorporate an empirical view on choice? I turn to Isaiah Berlin, who in his introduction to the *Essays on Liberty* responds to similar concerns:

> Finally one may ask what value is in liberty as such. Is it a response to a basic need of men, or only something presupposed by other fundamental demands? And further, is it an empirical question, to which psychological, anthropological, sociological, historical facts are relevant? Or is it a purely philosophical question, the solution of which lies in the correct analysis of our basic concepts, and does the answer to which the production of examples, whether real or imaginary, and not the factual evidence demanded by empirical enquiries, is sufficient and appropriate? . . . could it be the case that if the evidence of the facts should go against us, we should have to revise our ideas, or withdraw them altogether . . . ? Or is their authority shown by philosophical analysis which convinces us that indifference to freedom is abnormal, that is, offends against what we conceive of as being spe-

cifically human, or at least, fully human . . . ? To this it is sufficient, perhaps, to say that those who have ever valued
liberty for its own sake believed that to be free to choose, and
not to be chosen for, is an inalienable ingredient in what
makes human beings human.[5]

Berlin's position reflects a common liberal view, namely, that
the normative power of choice overwhelms any empirical input
into the question of its role in human society. But this argument
can be adjusted to accommodate the suggestion that a deeper and
more accurate understanding of "psychological, anthropological,
sociological, historical facts" can inform the theoretical argument
for choice. It can make the case for choice as an expression of freedom in a way that would support its proper implementation in social policy. Allowing research on the ways in which individuals
choose to inform normative theories about freedom could generate a powerful connection between theories of freedom and social
policies that can express and enhance that freedom.

The motivation for introducing these studies into the normative
debate on choice is not, as Berlin warns, to "revise our ideas, or
withdraw them altogether" but rather to create a more solid connection between the ideal of freedom and choice on the one hand,
and social policies that aim to implement it on the other. This connection, when it relies on a realistic perspective on the ways individuals choose, can prove to be a helpful tool for strengthening
choice in the arena of social policy making.

Normative theories of freedom and choice can benefit from utilizing a foundation in the empirical study of human behavior, particularly as it addresses rationality and choice. While normative
theories' relation to empirical data is not a clear and direct one, and
the history of philosophy is fraught with arguments about the justified disconnect between the descriptive and the prescriptive, the
"is" and the "ought," there is a case to be made for considering the
study of human behavior when structuring a normative theory of
public policy. If government—and public policy as the expression

of its intentions—are meant to shape society and direct it, theories and analyses of public policies can benefit from considering the psychology and sociology of human behavior as a factor in the structure and implementation of its policies. As far as normative theory is meant to inform government and public policy, as far as theories of justice aspire to affect the ways in which society is governed and its operations, the reflective equilibrium between the descriptive and the normative can prove to be a productive way of thinking about both.

The introduction of empirical research to the liberal-democratic conceptualizations of freedom and choice as attempted here suggests that the conditions of choice should be reconsidered if they are to satisfy the requirements of freedom. In other words, for individuals to be able to choose in a meaningful way, social policies should be designed in ways that maintain a principled commitment to freedom as a core value of democracy, while reflecting more directly actual processes of choice, rather than idealized notions of freedom or autonomy.

The main aim of this book is to analyze the landscape of choice both theoretically and from a policy perspective, and to provide a justificatory account of structured paternalism as a tool for enhancing opportunity and thus expanding the horizons of choice. The analysis includes both political and personal dimensions of choice, and culminates in a critical consideration of the role of education as a site where regulative policies and personal choice are both expressed and shaped.

In the next chapter I define and examine the concept of paternalism, and offer a modest defense of paternalism as a tool in social policy making. Chapter 3 considers the implications of this endorsement of paternalism to the area of intimate choices, including those taken about an individual's body and her sexual and familial relations. Chapter 4 considers paternalism as a practice unique to the relations of adults with children. It suggests that the differences between adults and children merit some special considerations for children, but that certain forms of paternalism can constitute appropriate dimensions of both adult-adult and adult-child relations.

The subsequent two chapters consider specific contexts in which social policies affect individuals' choice sets and the processes of decision making among those choices. Chapter 5 looks at choices about cultural affiliation and cultural, including religious, practices. Chapter 6 examines the unique case of choosing a school for one's child, where the considerations from previous chapters—on intimacy, family, and culture—coincide. The conclusion summarizes the view that structured paternalism, as exemplified in these areas of social interaction, can protect individuals from harm and enhance their opportunity to improve their well-being and their standing as civic equals by properly constructing their landscape of choice.

---— 2 —---

Why Paternalism Is Good for You

In the American public debate, freedom is often equated with choice, and this alignment represents a powerful influence on policy making. In both normative discussions and policy debates, choice is contrasted with paternalism, usually to the detriment of the latter. Policies that allow more personal choice—in education, health care, and other domains—are deemed more desirable and justifiable than ones categorized as paternalistic. This line of argument suggests that having choices and choosing are generally better than having institutional constraints; one knows better than the government what is in her best interest, and she is therefore entitled to pursue her preferences without paternalistic intervention, that is, without strict institutional directives constraining her decisions.

This chapter offers a critique of this view, and presents a defense of structured paternalism. I argue that paternalism, when properly constructed, can advance the values as well as policy aims of democratic institutions. The discussion in this chapter addresses key anti-paternalism arguments, namely, that paternalism is coercive, that it is suitable for children but not for adults, and that it is an affront to rationality or to autonomy. I defend paternalism as an approach that potentially enhances well-being and civic equality, when it is designed with a recognition of individual differences and of actual cognitive processes of personal decision making.

Structured paternalist policies can reorganize the landscape of choice, extending further opportunities to individuals.

The questions underlying the discussion of paternalism's merits and threats are, What are the justified limits on freedom? When is it justified for the government to subvert an individual's judgment and replace it with that of its policy makers? A discussion of paternalism thus requires an understanding of why this concept is important in the context of democratic theory and the practice of policy making.[1] Various authors begin their analysis of paternalism and its practices by suggesting that paternalism is insulting or demeaning. Joel Feinberg, for example, famously asserts that "the spontaneous repugnance toward paternalism (which I assume the reader shares with me) is well-grounded and supportable."[2] Counter to this common stance, I maintain that paternalism is an inevitable and indispensable aspect of social relations and of democratic policy making. It is important to discuss paternalism in the context of policy making not so much in order to identify its instances so as to argue against them and eradicate them, but rather so that paternalism can be instituted in properly justified forms to advance democratic aims, and in particular civic equality.

Civic equality (or equal standing as a citizen) is a main charge of a democratic society, and should serve as a central goal of its policy making. While this claim is widely accepted, pursuing it entails challenges to the prevailing rejection of paternalism. This is particularly the case for liberal scholars who reject paternalism on the basis of a combination of a strong belief in at least the potentiality of human excellence and a suspicion of state power as a potential form of coercion. Many liberal scholars challenge paternalism on this dual ground. They suggest that because all human beings are at least potentially autonomous, their conceptions of the good should be respected through extensive policies of nonintervention. In addition, liberals, like libertarians and others, are sometimes wary of the state's potential coercive power, and are thus quick to support limitations on the expressions of this power.

19

To respond to these concerns, I suggest a reconsideration of paternalism, through a more benevolent lens—one that might present its liberal-egalitarian dimensions in a way that makes them acceptable to some of its critics. First, desirable paternalist policies (as defined and discussed later) assume that various needs must be addressed before individuals in contemporary democracies are able to reach a civic minimum, one that would allow them to participate as equals in democratic processes.[3] In this way, civic equality is tied to individuals' well-being, and not primarily to their autonomy. Paternalist policies can construct choice sets in the context of the distribution of goods (such as savings, health care, and education) in ways that allow individuals to better pursue their preferences and aspirations. Subsequently, these policies support individuals' well-being and help them reach the threshold conditions necessary for civic equality. Note that the basic conditions for well-being that are at the foundations of civic equality are a threshold rather than a scheme of equal distribution. The details of the threshold conditions for civic equality or a minimally decent life can be disputed, and my intention is not to detail them here; rather, I suggest that whatever their exact details might be, it should be considered reasonable—in fact, it would often be inevitable—to pursue their implementation through paternalist policies. Paternalistic policies are sometimes necessary for securing the basic conditions of civic equality, and, through securing these basic conditions, provide individuals with an appropriate context for making meaningful choices.

For this argument, a preliminary working definition of justified paternalism in the context of democratic social policy would describe it as an attempt to improve the circumstances or well-being of others while keeping in mind their inferred needs, including the threshold conditions of civic equality and the expansion of opportunity.

In the following section, I discuss some anti-paternalism arguments and weigh them in light of this definition.

Anti-paternalism

Let me begin my defense of paternalism with a strong anti-paternalist statement, from Isaiah Berlin's opening remarks to his *Five Essays on Liberty*:

> Kant . . . denounced paternalism, since self-determination is precisely what it obstructs; even if indispensable for curing certain evils at certain times, it is, for opponents of tyranny, at best a necessary evil; as are all great accumulations of power as such. Those who maintain that such concentrations are sometimes required to remedy injustices, or to increase the insufficient liberties of individuals or groups, tend to ignore or play down the reverse of the coin: that much power (and authority) is also, as a rule, a standing threat to fundamental liberties . . . all paternalistic governments, however benevolent, cautious, disinterested and rational, have tended, in the end, to treat the majority of men as minors, or as being too often incurably foolish or irresponsible; or else maturing so slowly as not to justify their liberation at any clearly foreseeable date (which, in practice, means at no definite time at all). This is a policy which degrades men, and seems to me to rest on no rational or scientific foundation, but, on the contrary, on a profoundly mistaken view of the deepest human needs.[4]

Berlin is suggesting that paternalism is to be rejected for two main reasons, one structural, the other psychological. The first is the concern that paternalism is bound to generate coercive relations between the state and the individual, and support an intrusion of the state into areas where individual rights should reign: "much power (and authority) is also, as a rule, a standing threat to fundamental liberties." The second critique of paternalist policies Berlin raises is that they are based on a false view of human psychology, one that regards adults as children, and fails to see the

21

strong capacities (and aspirations) of human beings to reason and to make autonomous choices.

My response to this twofold attack on paternalism—characteristic of the contemporary debate on the topic—attempts to defend paternalism as a component of social policy. In what follows, (1) I briefly consider the suggestion that paternalism is necessarily coercive, and (2) I criticize the suggestion that paternalism is an affront to adulthood, either because it (2.1) rejects rationality or because it (2.2) undermines autonomy. In conclusion, I establish the possible merits of structured paternalism for policy making in a democracy.

1. Paternalism Equals Coercion

Advocating the avoidance of (or strong limitation on) paternalistic coercion is tightly linked to an argument for freedom, and for freedom of choice. Choice, in turn, is associated with non-paternalist policies. Controlling one's choice making is assumed to offer a host of goods, including the opportunity to discover one's true preferences, and a sounder legitimacy of the state.

Much of this anti-paternalist argument dates back to Mill, who alongside Kant informs most contemporary anti-paternalist approaches. Mill construes paternalism as the nonconsensual exercise of power over the individual for his own good. This lack of consent makes an action or a policy unjustified (except in cases where consent is unfeasible; I return to this exception later). But even if this argument is accurate, would paternalism necessarily entail coercive measures that would significantly undermine personal freedom, thus compromising democracy? Moreover, in the context of an organized state, what is the alternative? The literature on paternalism, both critical and carefully sympathetic, establishes a direct connection between paternalism and coercion. For example, over three decades ago in his landmark article "Paternalism," Gerald Dworkin presented an argument against an absolute ban on paternalism.[5] He states, "By paternalism I shall understand roughly the interference with a person's liberty of action justified by reasons referring exclusively to the welfare, good, happiness, needs, interests, or values of the person being coerced."[6] The focus on coercion as a key aspect of paternalism is widespread, and it is the cause for much of the suspicion paternalism raises among scholars and the public. I believe this focus on coercion is mistaken, both because coercion in these contexts is not necessary, and because it is not necessarily evil. Let me explain these two points in turn.

First, paternalism need not be coercive. If paternalism is a metaphor borrowing from the relations between parents and their children, these relations can take many forms. The direction that parents provide their children, including the ways in which parents limit their children's choices to make their decisions more in line with what the parents perceive as desirable, is not necessarily coercive in its intent, structure, or delivery. In response to similar points made by his critics,[7] Dworkin later restructured his definition, arguing that paternalism should be understood more broadly as interference, ranging from reasoning to exerting force, with a person's autonomy.[8] Likewise, in their recent and widely debated work, Cass Sunstein and Richard Thaler maintain that paternalism need not be coercive, stating that "a policy counts as 'paternalistic' if it is selected with the goal of influencing the choices of affected parties in a way that will make those parties better off."[9] This latter definition, I believe, better describes contemporary paternalist policies, and it redeems paternalism to some extent from the accusation of being coercive.

Understanding that in many cases paternalism may not be coercive can assist a more proper identification of paternalist policies and distinguish justified from unjustified ones and, in this way, ease much of the suspicion that the term generates. A policy can be paternalist without being coercive, for example, by establishing default rules but allowing individuals to opt out.[10] Public educational campaigns, such as those launched against domestic violence or for abstinence until marriage, are another example of paternalist policies—policies that are designed with the others' well-being or inferred needs and values in mind, "for their own good," but without direct coercive measures. These noncoercive paternalist policies frame individual choice in a particular way or direct individuals to develop certain preferences. They do not, however, preclude individuals from choosing other options, and they do not impose a particular choice. As these examples show, paternalist interventions can happen alongside more strict or coercive actions such as criminalization (as in the case of domestic violence) where a public campaign supplements the criminal law. This joint paternalist action, legal and public-educational, represents an acknowledgment of the law's limited reach into the intimate sphere, as will be discussed in the next chapter. Paternalist public campaigns can also take place without additional coercive measures, as in the case of discouraging premarital sexual activity; in this case, the public (or the local government) takes a moral position and promotes it, but does not coercively impose it, nor does it penalize for failure to adhere.

A second reason why the assumed connection between paternalism and coercion is mistaken is that much of the literature on paternalism ignores, or interprets unfavorably, paternalism's motivational focus on the well-being of the policy's objects. Regulatory policies, from laws to binding institutional practices, restrict individual choice and thus can be described as paternalist. Coercion by restriction is common enough in institutional design and legal regulation that few policies would merit the title "non-paternalistic." Sunstein and Thaler recognize this when they correctly describe paternalism as "unavoidable."[11] An attempt to eradicate paternalism, if it is equated with the power of the state, would amount to eradicating the state, perhaps leaving a "night watchman state," as suggested by Robert Nozick and other libertarians.[12] The argument that the night watchman state is the most extensive justifiable state is a sound argument, but its applicability is questionable, as is its desirability from the perspective of civic equality. Hence, if a more extensive state is the political starting point for the discussion of paternalism in policy making, paternalism cannot be rejected, and it must be acknowledged as an essential aspect of state function. Laws are paternalistic in restricting citizens' actions without their direct consent. Even if the citizens give their implied consent through their elected representatives, anti-paternalists may find the accumulation of legal restrictions and multiple levels of regulation offensive. But accepting that paternalism is part and parcel of the functioning of a liberal or liberal-egalitarian state can move the debate beyond this sense of offense, and into a more productive discussion of the distinction between desirable and undesirable paternalist policies.

Note that even if unavoidable, paternalism should not be assumed to necessarily consist of coercive and otherwise undesirable measures. In fact, if interference of some kind is inevitable, would individuals not reasonably prefer policies designed with their "welfare, good, happiness, needs, interests or values" in mind rather than with other aims, such as cost effectiveness? The motivational component of paternalism, which to some authors (like Seana Shiffrin) represents its more demeaning aspects, can be better interpreted as at least potentially a form of consideration of individuals' needs. When those are properly qualified and proven to potentially support well-being, civic equality, and the expansion of opportunities, they should at least not be offhandedly rejected as paternalist and thus coercive and undesirable.

Paternalism thus need not be rejected as coercive; in social policy as in workplace contexts, paternalism should be viewed as unavoidable. In its more desirable forms, paternalism consists of a dedication to advancing the good of individuals, and subsequently supporting their levels of civic equality by designing positive opportunities for them to be equal members of society and to pursue their goals.

However, the coercive nature of paternalism is not the only major objection to paternalist policies. A common anti-paternalist argument suggests that it would be demeaning, or infantilizing, to allow for paternalism to abound in a democratic society. In other words, paternalism is objectionable because it means that policy makers treat adult members of the community as if they were children. I next turn to this anti-paternalist argument.

2. Paternalism Is Good Only for Children

Another main point of contention many theorists have with paternalism has to do with its root in the word "pater," which relates paternalism with fatherhood. In the previous excerpt, Berlin warns against the tendency of paternalist governments to "treat the majority of men as minors." Paternalism's expression of a position of superiority over the adult agent on whose behalf a decision is being made, or a policy enacted, is deemed demeaning. An adult is assumed to be defined by her knowledge of what is in her best interest, and an attempt to limit her choices "for her own good" consequently strips her of the respect she is due as an adult. "Paternalism is of philosophic interest not because of the way parents legitimately relate to their children—indeed there is oddity in describing this conduct as 'paternalistic'—but rather because something like this practice is introduced into relations among adults. If our responses to adults mirror intrusive and solicitous parental responses to children we behave paternalistically."[13] And this paternalism, as the tone of this quote indicates, is unjustifiable. To limit an adult's choice set or coerce her, to treat her as a parent does a child, i.e., paternalistically, is unjustifiable because it denies her of her achieved status as an adult.

When, if ever, is it justified to treat an adult like a child? And how would "treating one like a child" and "treating one like an adult" manifest themselves? The strong tendency in the literature is to differentiate the two in a binary way, and to suggest that while it is often justified to treat children paternalistically, it is rarely, if ever, justified to treat healthy and capable adults that way.[14] This distinction is based on an often implicit Kantian assumption that children, like mentally ill and cognitively impaired adults, lack rationality and autonomy and thus cannot be regarded as agents in the full sense of the term.

The term "child," however, is itself contextual and can change in relation to different eras, cultures, and policies. Evolving from a child into an adult is not an on/off instance. Much like autonomy, maturity is a spectrum on which individuals evolve at different rates. Therefore, policies that consider maturity to be a precondition require some attention to detail, rather than deeming them justified or unjustified solely on the basis of their paternalist approach to children and the opposite toward adults.

Of course, policy requires some simplification in the way the state groups people together for the sake of regulating their behavior. For efficiency purposes, it makes sense to decide who is a child and, conversely, who is an adult in a dichotomous fashion for the purpose of legalizing and regulating criminal liability, consent, marriage, and other practices. The rationale for many policies based on this distinction between adults and children is the latter's need of protection. The democratic state regulates sexual conduct, alcohol consumption, driving, marrying, and working under a certain age, because children are perceived as requiring protection in these realms, partly because they are deemed unfit to make decisions autonomously and rationally in some of these areas.[15] Other practices like voting are restricted not because of children's need for protection, but because of their inferred lack of knowledge and rationality. The state further mandates and funds education among other reasons because children need external, professional guidance to assist with their development.[16]

But should this legal or formal dichotomy between adults and children affect all policies concerning adults? A common approach in the literature is to reject paternalism for adults because it is justified for children, under the assumption that paternalism is demeaning for adults because it suits a child. Many scholars reject paternalism as an affront to adulthood, as Peter de Marneffe expresses when he suggests critically that "some liberties have a special value in symbolizing the status of adulthood within our society, the freedom to marry for example" and therefore "it makes sense to think the government would treat us like children if it were to make our marital decisions for us."[17]

I would like to suggest that while paternalism toward children is often justified, it nonetheless may be suitable in various cases for adults as well. It is easy to find refutations to the suggestion that most people would feel humiliated or belittled by paternalistic relations and policies. For example, many professions and workplaces encourage formal and informal mentorship relations, which present many of the same characteristics as paternalistic ones. They are meant to support, direct, and change the behavior of individuals, in order to help them adjust to an environment that is new to them. The new employee or junior fellow in the workplace is commonly paired with a more senior or experienced colleague who can help her navigate the new terrain. In this way, her inferred needs—to get acquainted with the workplace, its culture and practices, and to be socialized to participate in it—guide the policy of mentorship; rather than treating the new employee as a rational adult who can handle the new environment (which she might be), these supportive structures aim to lead her in the right direction.

In the public sphere and in policy making, many paternalist policies are deemed justifiable even by some libertarians. From seat belts to quality assurance to mandatory car insurance, other considerations often trump anti-paternalism in both theory and practice. And rightfully so—endorsing paternalistic policies toward children signifies a view that children deserve special care and protection or that they could use direction in making choices that would be good for them. That does not mean that adults never need such treatment, or that treating them this way is necessarily demeaning. Food safety measures are good for everyone, even as they treat individuals as incapable of determining what to eat that would be good for them; seat belt laws express paternalism as they protect adults from harming themselves and others by carelessness. These and others are widely endorsed paternalist policies, in that they recognize the limitations on adults' rational decision making and work to direct all adults to choose wisely.

To summarize the argument so far, the widespread fixation on "treatment as an adult" misses significant positive aspects of the more complex relations that we should anticipate and benefit from as adults, and in particular as citizens. Paternalistic relations are reasonable components of the relations adults have with children, but they are also a reasonable aspect of some adult-adult relations, as well as a dimension of some justifiable policies. Paternalism understood as relevant to personal relations as well as to policy making and regulatory decision making should inform a critical discussion of its acceptable and unacceptable uses, how paternalistic relations can be legitimate, what might their benefits be for improving personal well-being and the social expansion of opportunities, and which expressions of paternalism should be amended or avoided.

Most anti-paternalist arguments that support the distinct treatment of adults and children focus on the Kantian argument that suggests adults are potentially or in effect rational and autonomous, whereas children lack these capabilities, thus justifying paternalist treatment of the latter but not the former. I now turn to consider these two related arguments.

2.1. Paternalism Is Good Only for Children, Because Adults Are Rational

"[A]ll paternalistic governments . . . have tended, in the end, to treat the majority of men . . . as being too often incurably foolish." Kantian thought as presented by Berlin states that respect for adulthood necessitates an acknowledgment by governing bodies of at least a potential for rationality in the citizenry, and as a consequence, trust in their judgment, and, thus, a rejection of paternalism. Paternalism is rejected in this argument because an adult is presumed to have the ability to make autonomous choices based on reasonable preferences and using deliberative and rational capacities. This general argument linking autonomy and rationality to adult capacities holds that a person becomes autonomous when certain aspects of her character are properly developed, allowing her to rationally evaluate her range of choices and choose among them according to her reasonable preferences.

This assumption of rationality, which has long dominated the paternalism discussion, is reconsidered today not only by pro-intervention egalitarians but also by libertarians like Sunstein and Thaler.[18] Their perspective is helpful here because it suggests a realistic, respectful approach to regulating choice—or acting paternalistically—which recognizes the inadequacies of the rationality assumption. While my argument is liberal-egalitarian rather than libertarian, I side with their suggestion that it is possible to affect individuals' behavior and guide their choices while still respecting their freedom of choice, and thus their adulthood.[19] The current argument, like the libertarian one, is informed by behavioral studies in the area of bounded rationality. Behavioral economics, a field of study whose groundwork was laid by Amos Tversky and Daniel Kahneman in their psychological studies of economic behavior,[20] characterizes adults' processes of decision making as quite dissimilar to its description in anti-paternalist arguments, as well as to common contemporary assumptions about agency in a democratic context. Rational decision making, as these studies make evident, is bounded by a host of factors, including often faulty intuition, context dependence, and strong risk aversion, which regularly trumps the attraction of an opportunity to benefit. In addition, a tendency to rely on heuristics in judgment frequently leads individuals to make choices that are not only deemed irrational and undesirable by external observers or professionals in the relevant field, but also would be deemed irrational and undesirable by the individual making the decision if she were taking into account all relevant and available information, including her own preferences.

Instances of these biases abound. Many people tend to compartmentalize financial decisions, allowing them to borrow (at a higher rate of interest) while they save (earning a lower rate of interest). Moreover, many individuals deviate from self-interest assumptions by preferring to share proceeds fairly rather than monopolize them. As bounded rationality literature would predict, empirical research shows that individuals tend to overestimate risk because of risk aversion or an overrepresentation of extreme cases of loss, because those are more memorable. At times they are too optimistic, and at other times they are overly pessimistic. Often, individuals do not have the information needed to make an informed decision, do not care or know how to acquire it, or they wrongly interpret it.

In addition, framing, or the way data are presented to individuals, has a massive effect on the outcome, or the decision they tend to make. In a famous 1982 study, one group of cancer patients was presented with a choice between surgery that provided a 90 percent chance of short-term survival and radiation therapy; another group was presented with the choice between surgery with a 10 percent chance of immediate mortality and radiation therapy. While the two sets of options are identical, the survival framework yielded a substantially higher preference for surgery over radiation than the mortality framework.[21]

Other factors beyond the heuristics of judgment and framing seem to undermine a strict notion of rational choosing. Some of these are relevant mostly to economic decision making, but many of them have consequences that should be taken seriously in the realm of public decisions and social policy making, beyond the economic domain.

These studies suggest that traditional distinctions between adults and children, ones that highlight the superior knowledge and judgment of adults as contrasted with children's lack of knowledge and poor judgment, become blurry when adults and their actual processes of decision making are considered. The assumed convergence between an agent's preferences and his action dates back to Vilfredo Pareto's "revealed preferences" theory, which assumes "that the subjective fact conforms perfectly to the objective fact"[22]—in other words, that preferences can be deduced from choices. This classical view crumbles in the face of empirical studies on choice.

Subsequently, Sunstein and Thaler, like Dan Ariely[23] and other contemporary researchers, call for a careful institution of default rules in areas like savings and (possibly) nutrition, an approach that encourages individuals in these contexts to make the right choice freely. The right choice here is identified by the assumption of a convergence between expert views on the issue—for example, what foods are good for one's health, or how much money one would need upon retirement—and the individual's inferred long-term goals and preferences, such as being healthy or retiring comfortably. Noticeably, these choices are made in the context of the workplace, and most of the suggested paternalistic interventions are instituted by employers for the purpose of promoting the long-term well-being of their employees, which is in the interest of employee and employer alike.[24]

But how is social policy to be affected by this acceptance of paternalism as an inevitable, often benign intervention in support of boundedly rational individuals? Maintaining a vision of libertarian values in the name of protecting individual liberties risks undermining the causes of individual well-being and civic equality in the phantom pursuit of independence from state intervention.[25] How would libertarian paternalism assist parents who face the choice between staying in a failing neighborhood school and transferring to another?[26] How would it assist individuals who are eligible for food stamps but for various reasons fail to register for the program, effectively choosing malnutrition for themselves and their children?[27] How would it inform policy makers in responding to such challenges? The answer must start with an attempt to structure institutions and regulations that affect individual behavior in ways that go beyond merely respecting individual freedom of choice (as libertarians aim to do). Beyond these freedoms, justifiably paternalist institutions and policies should uphold the core values that underlie freedom of choice, namely, respect for individual differences and a commitment to civic equality and individual well-being. Supporting the basic well-being of all individuals through developing relevant, accessible choice sets is a means for achieving civic equality. Policies that aim for this goal can signify respect for actual adults rather than for an idealized notion of adulthood. If adults are not rational in the classical sense, the aspect of the anti-paternalist argument that is based on respecting adults as rational agents is significantly weakened. Subsequently, paternalism gains grounds as a justified approach to social policy making.

Next I consider the twin anti-paternalist argument, namely, the argument from autonomy.

2.2. Paternalism Is Good Only for Children, Because Adults Are (Potentially) Autonomous

Kant's original concern about paternalism, as Berlin presents it, is that "self-determination is precisely what it obstructs." At the root of some anti-paternalist perspectives and sentiments lies the high value placed on autonomy as a key aspect of democratic citizenship and identity. Equal dignity is the basis for civic equality; civic equality, so the argument goes, is expressed through the equal opportunity all citizens have to shape their personal lives and the common future of society. Paternalism seems to stand in the way of this form of civic equality by tilting the balance between individual control and state intervention too far in the direction of the state, thus signifying a dwindling respect for individuals as authors of their own lives and of the public agenda.

Scholars who value autonomy can fall on either side of the paternalism discussion. Those who view autonomy as a given dimension of adult psychology focus their anti-paternalist argument on the demand to respect individuals' self-rule. On the other hand, those who view autonomy as an aspiration offer a perfectionist pro-paternalist argument that mandates autonomy-facilitating policies.

The first stance, advocating the rejection of paternalism out of respect for presumed autonomy, is represented by scholars such as Dworkin who, as mentioned earlier, relies on the acknowledgment of autonomy in his strong statement against coercion. Shiffrin, similarly, suggests that "paternalist doctrines and policies convey a special, generally impermissible, insult to autonomous agents."[28] She offers a motive-based characterization of paternalism that identifies paternalistic policies by the motivations of the agencies and agents who design and implement those policies. Policies that are aimed at affecting the agent's agency by substituting her judgment in matters that legitimately lie within her control with the presumably superior judgment of the policy maker are paternalistic and thus illegitimate, or at least undesirable and hard to justify.[29] This argument is based on an assumption of the superiority, or priority, of the individual's judgment over other judgments (such as experts' judgment), and its key dimensions were discussed critically in the previous section.

In a different take on the importance of autonomy for policy making, perfectionist scholars and others justify certain forms of paternalism by claiming that autonomy is an ideal trait rather than a given one. Thus, the democratic state is justified in intervening and directing individuals to choose in ways that would make them more autonomous—and thus less prone to paternalistic intervention—in the long run. Perfectionist scholars tend to justify certain forms of paternalism, which limit an individual's liberty and autonomy now, for the long-term gain of developing more autonomy and thus becoming eligible for more liberty in the future.

One of the strongest advocates of this line of argument is Joseph Raz, whose approach provides a benchmark for many discussions on liberty, autonomy, and authority.[30] Raz details a perfectionist argument for autonomy as the basis for liberty; he supports state coercion inasmuch as it is aimed to preclude immoral or otherwise unworthy choices, namely, choices that impede an agent's capacity for autonomy. Raz suggests that his version of liberalism deviates from most liberal accounts in that it embraces some forms of paternalism. While many liberals reject paternalism, he claims, they

accept safety and quality controls by state agencies, and for a good
reason—they constitute protection without coercion. Paternalism,
Raz contends, is varied enough to merit a complex discussion and
does not yield itself to overall endorsement or rejection.

This seems to be a reasonable starting point for liberals, whether
their main commitment is autonomy, liberty, welfare, or equality.
Raz's main concern is with the preservation of autonomy—the
basic component of his doctrine of freedom and a necessary aspect
of the good life as he depicts it. Some instances of paternalism do
not impede autonomy and may even promote the development of
abilities necessary for leading an autonomous life. "Respect for
persons," Raz says, "requires concern for their well-being" and the
assignment of "a central role to the agent's own activities in shaping
his well-being." This view requires "that people should be allowed
to freely create their own lives."[31] This autonomy-based view of
morality thus leaves room for instances of paternalism that support the development of autonomous capacities. It "looks to governments to take positive action to enhance the freedom of their
subjects."[32]

Thus, Raz's perfectionist line of pro-paternalism supports limited forms of paternalism in the hope of relinquishing those once
further autonomy and liberty are achieved. While I agree with Raz
and others that paternalism need not be rejected indiscriminately,
I disagree with the key role assigned to autonomy in their understanding of the good life, and in particular in its use for the justification of desirable forms of paternalism. Perfectionists regard autonomy as a good that underlies most of what is valuable about
human life. But a commitment to cultural value differences, including the protection of those who do not espouse autonomy as a
primary value, poses a problem to this perfectionist form of prioritizing autonomy. Ronald Dworkin rejects what he calls critical paternalism, which "supposes that coercion can sometimes provide
people with lives that are better than the lives they now think
good."[33] He thus rejects paternalism as an expression of positive
liberty, or as an attempt to enhance the endorsement of valuable

aims by individuals who do not internally value these aims. To follow this argument, how can autonomy be prioritized as a foundational value that all should cherish, when there are various ways of life—religious and other—that do not endorse autonomy and possibly even reject it? The perfectionist endorsement of autonomy, which at first blush seemed to be aimed at providing freedom to all, suddenly seems authoritarian, imposing a single value on all to endorse.

It may be possible for some perfectionists to respond by suggesting that autonomy may not be the single value underlying all versions of the good life, but rather defining autonomy as one good among many goods, and not a necessary condition either for the good life or for good citizenship. While many individuals value autonomy as a key component of their well-being, self expression, civic standing, and other goods, others may have second-order preferences that do not give priority to autonomy. For the purpose of designing policies that relate to individual well-being, autonomy does not necessarily need to be given priority over other values. Individuals may value their various affiliations, traditions, and habits as much as they value their status as autonomous agents and the choices conferred on them as a result. The push to "encourage the adoption of valuable ends and discourage the pursuit of base ones"[34] is based on a rejection of the multiplicity of aims and conceptions of the good, and the myriad ways those are developed. In other words, the fact that individuals may value their autonomy is not by itself a sufficient reason to prioritize it in policy making above other values individuals hold.[35] In a democratic society, regulation and policy making should focus on the opportunities that advance main democratic aims, specifically well-being and civic equality, rather than on particular ones like autonomy.

In sum, both pro-paternalist and anti-paternalist views on autonomy fall short of providing a sound argument on the role of paternalism in policy making because they rely on a thin and inadequate psychological view of the individual, and because they fail to take into account collective normative goals beyond the development of autonomy.

So far I have critically considered a number of challenges to paternalism and presented the potential value of paternalism as a tool for social policy making. In particular, I have suggested that paternalist policies that aim to enhance individual well-being and maintain a commitment to civic equality should be seen as justifiable from a democratic perspective. I now turn to look more closely at this pro-paternalist argument and consider its consequences for theory and policy.

Why Paternalism Is Good for You

Pro-paternalist arguments often defend paternalism by presenting it as a limited-time mechanism for avoiding harmful decisions or for developing certain personal traits, first among them autonomy. In such cases, pro-paternalistic arguments tend to focus on particular groups or on limited, localized instances. Paternalism in this form is justified toward children, the mentally ill, or drug addicts; it is justified when one is about to cause oneself irreversible or unintended harm, or when it can support the realization of one's existing (stated or inferred) preferences.

Mill provides us with the basic version of both primary justifications for paternalism. First, paternalism is to be accepted if it is practiced on an individual whose judgment is deemed impaired. In this case, the individual is about to unknowingly cause harm to herself, and the patronizing agent—another person or the state—rightfully exercises power over her, even against her will, to avoid that harm. The second justified form of paternalism according to Mill is when the harm one is about to cause will result in the alienation of his liberty (as with selling oneself into slavery), such that it can properly be said that he will no longer be a self-determining or self-governing agent. Beyond these two types of case, Mill suggests that paternalist policies are to be rejected as unjustified coercive intrusions on individual freedom.

Echoing this vision, Dennis Thompson lists three criteria for justified paternalism: impaired judgment, temporary and reversible intervention, and preventing a serious and irreversible harm.[36] In a similar Millian fashion, Feinberg has famously justified what he refers to as soft or weak paternalism: "Soft paternalism holds that the state has the right to prevent self-regarding harmful conduct . . . when but only when that conduct is substantially nonvoluntary, or when temporary intervention is necessary to establish whether it is voluntary or not."[37] Dworkin argues in defense of what he calls volitional paternalism, which "supposes that coercion can sometimes help people achieve what they already want to achieve."[38]

Both traditional defenses of paternalism—impaired judgment and protection of liberty or autonomy—miss the point. If paternalism is to advance the twin aims of well-being for individuals and the expansion of opportunities that support civic equality, it must not be designed in a way that would discriminate against a particular group or be perceived as indicating incapacity. If my argument that paternalism is a helpful approach for realizing public policies in an equitable and socially conscious way is correct, then paternalism should be directed toward all in the instances in which it is justified. In other words, it should not be directed toward the "other"—children, the mentally ill, those unable to realize their professed goals, the poor—but toward all citizens equitably. The decision about when paternalism is justified should mostly be based on generalized rather than specific contexts, and it should aim to advanced generalized rather than tailored aims.

Paternalism is not justified merely by the extent to which it is under time constraints, or by the extent to which it develops autonomy or averts immediate harm. In addition, advocating for paternalism in limited settings, such as paternalism by employers (the way Sunstein and Thaler do), may be helpful but is not sufficient. Paternalist policies are justified when they advance the public good of civic equality, as related to the private good of enhanced well-being and expanded opportunities. In other words, justified paternalism advances well-being, which is part of the conditions for achieving the threshold of civic equality, by providing opportunities and goods one needs in order to live a minimally decent life and to advance her chosen goals, consistent with others' civic equality. This well-being can be advanced through policies that limit or otherwise regulate one's choices as well as through policies that expand the set of choices available, taking into account existing knowledge about the ways in which individuals tend to choose, and the forces that affect these choices both externally and internally (i.e., socially and psychologically).

From a liberal-democratic perspective, as well as from a liberal-egalitarian one, it seems reasonable to endorse an approach to social policy that recognizes the reality of human abilities and limitations, and design institutions and policies that enable society and the individuals within it to reach their goals and improve their overall well-being. This form of structured paternalism need not be infantilizing or demeaning. It would reflect recognition of the moral realities of human diversity of aims and preferences, and of bounded rationality in advancing these aims. It would further reflect an endorsement of an approach to social policy that responds to this reality. Structured paternalism recognizes that informed desire accounts of personal welfare, or the identification of an agent's welfare with her rational preferences, fail to acknowledge the complexity of desires, wishes, first- and second-order preferences, and external influences on the makeup of individual preferences. Such assumptions of rationality do not consider the intricate ways in which individuals' varied preferences are communicated to others, and even to the agent herself. Therefore, using these accounts of personal preference as the basis for political and economic theories or as guidelines for social policies would be misguided. Another basis is needed upon which to establish social policies, and the current suggestion is that structured paternalism can offer such an alternative.

How can a justified paternalistic policy be differentiated from a demeaning, undemocratic, or otherwise unjustified one? Stephen Darwall suggests rational care theory, or inferred preferences based on the agent's good, as a differentiating factor for justified welfare policies.[39] As Darwall too rejects the notion that a person's good is subjective, his vision shares the current understanding of well-being (or welfare) as normative. A normative account of well-being necessarily has paternalistic components if paternalism is understood as acting on the inferred needs of another, for her own sake. Recognizing the diversity of human ends leaves policy makers and scholars with the need to define paternalism in a substantial and inclusive way. It justifies policies that steer individuals to directions that support their well-being, without being coercive or demeaning, and without being discriminatory.

Paternalism is thus justifiably practiced when it takes into account an individual's well-being when designing a relevant choice set for her and informing her of her options, thereby steering the agent through noncoercive measures in the direction of those choices which are assumed to best satisfy her inferred preferences and needs. It is labeled structured paternalism because it organizes choice sets and access to opportunities through crafting policies that enable, and rarely coerce, individuals to express their diverse preferences within these structures.

This description is broad, but it rejects paternalist policies that are discriminatory against the "other"—immigrants, the poor, the elderly—and which thus fail to support civic equality. It rejects paternalist policies that provide an inadequate range of choices—either too broad or too narrow—thereby failing to respect individual differences, as well as those policies that fail to inform individuals of their choices and to solicit their participation in choosing where this is warranted.

Some possible examples of paternalist policies that would not be justified under this broad pro-paternalist argument are discriminatory policies that effectively prohibit certain individuals from choosing a suitable form of schooling for their children while allowing others to choose. It rejects policies that effectively favor the affluent or the devout. Other paternalist policies that do not correspond with the guidelines of structured paternalism are those that limit access through creating an unreasonably broad choice set, for example, by offering a wide range of health care options about which the cost of information gathering is prohibitive for many individuals, thus expanding the choice set in ways that impede the achievement of a threshold well-being and civic equality. In other instances, a broader range of choices would be more adequate for advancing well-being and civic equality, as long as it included proper procedures for informing individuals of their choices, along with well-designed default rules (where appropriate).

Structured paternalism in this form is further justified because of its relations to responsibility. For many advocates of choice, particularly libertarian ones, choice suggests a capability to express a preference for a reason, and to live with the consequences. Structured paternalism offers an opportunity to share the responsibility for one's actions with the state. This shared responsibility is a justified dimension of structured paternalist policies, because the state's role in structuring one's choice set is inevitable. As suggested at the beginning of this chapter, paternalism is, to a large extent, unavoidable; the state cannot but construct the choice set available to individuals in many contexts. One's circumstances of birth, including her gender, race, class, (dis)ability, and cognitive capacity, affect her opportunities. They affect it for reasons that are dependent on further conditions beyond her choice, such as current gender and race relations in society, or social views about certain talents and disabilities. An individual in contemporary democratic societies is free to choose various facets of her life, but she can do it only against the backdrop of her natural and social endowment. The state thus is inherently implicated in the allocation of opportunities. It should therefore share the responsibility of an individual's choices with her. It should further take an active role in equalizing and expanding opportunities rather than leaving it to individuals to make up their life story, under the false pretense that they are doing it as free and equal members of society.

A justified paternalistic policy, or structured paternalism, is one that takes into account individuals' diverse preferences as well as the internal and external challenges they face in realizing their preferences. It takes into account the variety of burdens that challenge individuals' well-being and make them effectively less than civic equals. In addition, structured paternalism attempts to provide a productive range of opportunities to all individuals, and particularly those who have been previously marginalized or who are facing the greatest challenges on their way to achieving civic equality. And it would aim to uphold respect for a wide variety of choices individuals make, while maintaining a commitment to direct them toward ones that can make their lives work best in the context of their values. Simply providing more choices does not necessarily improve individuals' opportunities to make choices that are good for them, as they would judge for themselves. The mere range of options within a choice set is insufficient to determine whether individuals are free, whether they are treated as civic equals, or whether their well-being is served. Upholding a commitment to freedom and to civic equality entails a support for paternalism that is less coercive and more regulatory, allowing for policies that aim to inform individuals of available choice sets, expand the range of options when needed, and frame them in ways that would increase their availability and the likelihood of individuals choosing the most productive ones. A discussion of policies that are aimed at improving the well-being of individuals or protecting them from harmful choices should thus not shy away from defending the paternalist presentation of a choice set that promotes a limited, broad enough set of options deemed to provide a better chance for individuals to flourish as civic equals.

— 3 —

THE REGULATION OF INTIMACY

THE PREVIOUS CHAPTER CONCLUDED that structured paternalism and interventions aimed at regulating individual conduct should not be rejected solely on the ground that they impede freedom. Justifiable forms of structured paternalism should be instituted through policies which, if carefully crafted, support civic equality and well-being through the structured expansion of opportunities. In this chapter, I look into one of the most difficult areas for implementing this argument, namely, the (de)regulation of intimate conduct. By "intimate conduct" I refer to the various ways in which an individual develops a sense of bodily integrity as well as the way she expresses herself through close and ongoing relations. This area of intimate conduct presents a challenge to any pro-paternalist argument, including the current one, because common anti-paternalist sentiments (and some of the anti-paternalist arguments) proliferate in this context. These include arguments about privacy rights and personal identity, which join the concerns regarding state coercion and the impeding of freedom to reject many paternalist interventions in the sphere of intimate self-expression and relations. This chapter considers the modes of regulating intimate conduct that are justified under the suggested framework of structured paternalism.

How, if ever, should the state regulate intimate conduct? Ever since John Locke drew a line in the sand by the household gate and declared that the government should not cross it, the liberal state has been repeatedly invited to pass this threshold and enter what was formerly known as the private sphere. Feminist critics suggest that protecting vulnerable members of the family from abuse and exploitation justifies breaching the line separating public from private.[1] Many critics who are concerned about vulnerability within the family advocate the use of legal tools to protect those vulnerable members, and thus to intervene in, and regulate, intimate relations. But the proliferation of legal interventions in the intimate sphere is a form of crude paternalism that goes against the aim defended in the previous chapters of supporting well-being and civic equality through the structuring of desirable choice contexts. The criminal legal system is an insufficient and often inappropriate tool for regulating intimate choices. Those should indeed be regarded as part of the state's jurisdiction or responsibility, contrary to the Lockean and classical liberal perspective; but structured paternalism should not be confined to legal tools when responding to choices made in the intimate sphere. Paternalist interventions, aimed at affecting individuals' decisions and actions, are justified in the intimate sphere when they are designed with both freedom and equality in mind. In other words, policies that affect intimate conduct should reflect respect to the plurality of aims and visions of the good life, of which intimate life is often a constitutive part, while still delineating a realm of desirable choices. Maintaining a wide range of opportunities for individuals to take advantage of, while supporting a productive process of choosing and a limited range of possible outcomes—barring the most destructive possibilities—is a way to express and uphold this respect. The state should thus minimize its legal interference in citizens' intimate lives and focus on more subtle ways to provide a structured context of choice. Most crucially, the state should offer forms of support and prevention in this sphere, to help individuals avoid destructive choices and thus support their well-being, a goal that can often be advanced by providing appropriate opportunities and choices, rather than by using punitive measures.

There is a relatively broad agreement in the literature that criminal measures are often inappropriate for dealing with certain instances of intimacy. Whether the state should criminalize any consensual form of adult sexual conduct is a point of heated debate between liberals and natural law advocates,[2] where the former defend a right to privacy over one's sexual preferences, and the latter uphold a "natural" normative order according to which (potential) procreation marks the legitimacy of sexuality. Outside the natural law tradition, however, the idea that consensual adult sexual behavior should not be criminalized or otherwise publicly regulated is mostly indisputable. I would like to argue for the extension of the immunity of consensual sex beyond its current limits and to apply it to other aspects of intimacy.

One such aspect would be most cases of domestic violence. When dealing with domestic violence—after properly acknowledging the problem—the state should in most cases focus its attention and resources on prevention, support for the victim or survivor and guidance for the perpetrator, rather than on prosecution. This approach should mostly substitute, and in some cases supplement or modify, the current legal and other formal regulatory institutions. It should be used in other intimate crossroads and in instances of vulnerability. In this way, individuals as well as society can benefit from a structured paternalist approach of prevention and support, more than they could benefit from formal regulation based on legal constraints and legal enforcement, prosecution, and punishment.

The argument in this chapter proceeds as follows. First, I differentiate intimacy from privacy, and the regulation of intimacy from privacy rights. Second, I engage current legal literature on intimacy to provide an overview of the strengths and weaknesses of responding legally to intimate conduct. Third, I suggest an alternative form of state regulation of intimacy, which is based on the argument for structured paternalism.

45

Intimacy and Privacy

Contrary to the common tendency in contemporary literature, I refrain from relating to intimacy through the prism of the right to privacy. Because I argue that the regulation of intimate conduct in structured paternalist ways is a unique case within the general framework of structured paternalism, I first explain why intimacy should be regarded as distinct from privacy, in ways that construct it as a special case.

The private sphere comprises a variety of aspects of human life, and its contents are continuously debated and updated. As one legal commentator famously noted, the private sphere could be described as "residual" [3]—whatever is left over after every matter that is legitimately public has been subtracted. [4] Hannah Arendt termed the historical private sphere as the shadowy interior of the household, where matters of the body and its needs were addressed— matters with undeniably lower value than that of public matters. [5] The private sphere is conceived in the political literature as consisting of religious and ethical commitments, economic activities, and the daily needs of life (sexuality, reproduction, and care for weak members of the family). [6] Each of these content matters of the private sphere was challenged by legal action or theoretical scrutiny, and there are arguments for the inclusion of each of these aspects in the public sphere. [7]

The most prominent reason for transferring a specific issue from the private to the public sphere, hence opening it to public scrutiny and legal regulation, is the harm principle. John Stuart Mill defined this principle, claiming that "the individual is not accountable to society for his actions, in so far as these concern the interests of no person but himself." [8] Liberal and libertarian theories have used the harm principle as the basic precept marking the borders of the private sphere. Legal and political debates have refined the definition of the private sphere from a spatial area consisting mainly of the house and personal property—including a man's family—to a sphere whose boundaries were defined conceptually around the notion of rights.

These developments turned the harm principle into a prominent rationale for banning what was previously regarded as personal immoral behavior.[9] It is widely used by conservative authors and politicians to pull out of the private sphere behaviors such as sexual conduct (mainly homosexuality), alcohol consumption, and other "moral offenses." The harm principle is used differently by radical authors, who demand further intervention of the state in harms to weak members of society or the family, in cases of oppression, harassment, and exploitation.

The rise of the harm principle has enabled the relocation of an array of private behaviors and choices to the public sphere, and has reframed the private sphere as a space where regulation may be partial and less intrusive but where still most aspects can be legally mandated. The "rapid shift in our conception of privacy"[10] and the ongoing cultural negotiation on the distinction between public and private have vast personal and political consequences. Some authors, "friends of privacy,"[11] have attempted to secure an unregulated private space by arguing for a right to privacy.

The attempt to protect the private sphere by reference to a "right to privacy" does not guard it from legal and public regulation. The use of the language of rights maintains the law as the primary adjudicator of the private sphere. From Samuel Warren and Louis Brandeis's notable 1890 article,[12] to the voluminous literature on privacy that was written ever since, discussions of privacy are mostly aimed at interpreting the scope and effects of the right to privacy. The choices made in the private sphere are described as part of one's life that should be free from state intervention; in the famous words of Thomas Cooley in 1888, it is the kind of choices about which we all have "the right to be let alone."[13] Later it was interpreted as the right to be free from intrusion,[14] the demand to exclude outsiders,[15] an expectation not be watched, derived from respect to one's autonomy,[16] and a concern for limited accessibility.[17]

Many legal and political scholars have attempted to define the right to privacy, failing to reach a consensus on its contents and desired forms of implementation. In fact, the United States Supreme Court seems to have given up on the concept of the right to privacy, and since 1992 started using the term "liberty" to substitute it, discussing "the realm of liberty in which the government may not enter."[18] What these conceptualizations of nonintervention come up to is at best a sphere of negative liberty, which does not support but rather abandon the individual to her choices and their outcomes. It does not in itself preserve a sphere of intimate acts and choices; neither does it exclude destructive choices. It assumes a universal preference and capacity to make choices one can argue for and maintain, or at least benefit from; it thus ignores the cognitive and other limitations on intimate decision making (which they share with choices made in other areas), as well as their sometimes irrational, revisable, and tentative nature.

Negative liberty is not enough to support a sphere where both diversity of aims and individual uniqueness can be developed, supported, and celebrated. The language of rights along with legal protection, embedded in a universal notion of personhood and personal interests, cannot provide a refuge from the universality that is the mark of the public sphere. This critical view need not amount to a vision of positive liberty in the private sphere, one that would mandate a perfectionist outcome, a prescribed way of leading a good private life. These concerns regarding negative liberty as the response of the state to the intimate sphere point to the need to rethink intimate choices and how they are regulated. Structured paternalism offers a reasonable response, as it provides a delineation of desirable choice sets and processes that support choice making.

Intimate choices are a key way in which individuals develop and express their personal identities; they are also a space where many forms of oppression and suffering take place. The need to maintain a free space for identity development clashes with the suggestion that individuals do not always manage to develop their identities in ways that maintain both their own well-being and the well-being of others with whom they are intimately connected. If intimate choices, for better or worse, influence the ways in which a person develops and expresses her identity, then the concept of rights in itself holds little promise for implementing procedures for supporting identity formation or the exercise of a variety of lifestyles. This is the case both conceptually and practically. On the conceptual level, the notion of rights, with the universality it endorses, can hardly reflect the plurality of ends that a just democracy must recognize, within the intimate sphere and beyond it. Rights, like laws, can barely respond to the multiplicity and depth of identities as they are developed and expressed through intimate choices.

Moreover, "rights create an illusion of justice; merely 'having a right' means very little in practice"[19] if one does not have the means—material, emotional, educational, and other—to put the right into effect. That is true about choices generally, especially in the context of social policies that allow individuals to choose but do not offer them the means to make informed choices, thus failing to turn choices into opportunities.

While rights are a plausible social and legal tool for implementing democratic justice and civic equality, they are inappropriate for responding to the more nuanced and personal challenges of the intimate sphere. When allocated on an equal basis, rights can serve as a baseline for the political and judicial systems to preserve a just basic structure to society. But as they proliferate, their effects are less predictable. In a sense, the constituting conceptions of the privacy debate—the harm principle, the private sphere, and the right to privacy—have collapsed from the burden of overuse and multiple interpretations. Rather than offering yet another interpretation of these conceptions that would allow them to be employed in regulating intimacy, I suggest a different conception of the state's role in the context of these relations, based on describing their unique role as identity-based, vastly diverse, and deeply entrenched aspects of an individual's self-perception. The intimate sphere, I suggest, cannot accommodate the language of rights, including the right to privacy. This language fails to describe satisfactorily the motivations, conceptions, and choices that constitute intimacy. Consequently, social (personalized, contextual) rather than legal (rights-based, universal, mandated) tools are to be used as means of regulation in the intimate domain. I now turn to contrast the two types of intervention tools, and to consider the shortcomings of applying legal tools to the regulation of intimacy.

Institutionalizing Intimacy: A Legal Response to the Debate

In her book *Regulating Intimacy*, Jean Cohen searches for a way to "shift attention away from the fruitless debate over regulation versus deregulation of intimate relationship" and to offer "possibilities other than the unattractive choice between privacy or equality, autonomy or responsibility."[20] She presents a new legal paradigm, which is designed to respond to the debate on privacy rights.

Cohen criticizes the liberal paradigm as based on archaic justifications, and the welfare paradigm as emphasizing outcomes, therefore infringing upon liberty and autonomy. As a substitute for these common legal paradigms, Cohen suggests an alternative: the reflexive legal paradigm. This paradigm essentially replicates the legal framework of the liberal one, without the "defunct theoretical baggage" of foundationalism, essentialism, or the assumption of a natural ordering of privacy. It is based on an acknowledgment of the social construction of autonomy, identity, and sexuality. According to Cohen, the reflexive paradigm can accommodate both autonomy and regulation. It thus dissolves the requirement to choose between equality and liberty in the realm of privacy rights.

This new legal approach is in effect a meta-paradigm, which allows courts and lawmakers to alternate between forms of regulation while acknowledging "contextual differences and ethical multiplicity."[21] It rests on the idea that "regulated self-regulation" can "steer self-regulation in the right direction" in the domain of private relations. Cohen assures her readers that opting for self-regulation does not in effect entail privatization because it rests on "clearly defined legislative goals."[22] These goals, however, do not amount to designing outcomes—thus avoiding the infringement of autonomy—for they are principles or procedures rather than well-defined choices.

The reflexive legal paradigm "was initially conceived as a potential alternative to two competing models of legal regulation,"[23] which emerge from the liberal and the welfarist theoretical approaches. Gunther Teubner originally suggested the reflexive paradigm as a response to the ills of this liberal, formalistic legal approach and the goal-oriented forms of state intervention, which characterize the welfare approach. Teubner's basic intuition was that "regulatory policies today are only likely to prove effective if they limit themselves to specifying procedures and basic organizational norms geared toward fostering self-regulation within distinct spheres of social activity."[24] While structured paternalism does not focus on legal procedures, it shares with Teubner the preference for regulatory policies that direct rather than coerce individuals. Cohen, despite her critique of Teubner's approach, follows this argument and applies it to the private sphere by rejecting the dichotomous choice between "the status-based public ordering" of intimacy, which is "sexist and unjust,"[25] and the privatization and deregulation of intimacy. Focusing on "the new privacy rights," namely, intimate relationship and intimate (sexual) decisions, Cohen argues that such relations deserve constitutional protection in the form of preserving decisional autonomy of the actors involved. She argues that these rights do not threaten the substance of the family, nor do they turn personal relations into contractual ones. Cohen rejects the communitarian as well as the feminist critique[26] of the new privacy rights. She regards the new privacy rights as protections "against the terrible effects of unwarranted trust and dependency." Marriage, she claims, is not turned into a contractual economic relation by the criminalization of spousal violence or by the extension of decisional autonomy to reproductive decisions. Rather, these developments "bring moral principles of justice to bear on intimate associations by acknowledging the individuality, legal standing, personal autonomy and civic equality of all adult family members." If some feminists and communitarians frown when reading this description, Cohen does not try to appease them: the new privacy rights, she says, "institutionalize the basic principles of mutual respect—nonviolence, bodily integrity, nondomination, nonexploitation—in the intimate domain."[27] In this sense, self-regulation is both assumed and supported in the domain of intimate relations.

Self-regulation as a policy goal assumes that some choices are better than others, or at least that some choices are clearly undesirable, an assumption that I share with Cohen (and Teubner). Contrary to her view, though, structured paternalism emphasizes that (1) it is not emotions but actions that should be regulated, and (2) tools beyond those available to the criminal justice system are needed in order to properly respond to intimate relations.

To clarify the first point, consider the institutionalization of mutual respect. This aim is practically unfeasible to legislate and regulate, but it is also morally undesirable as a goal of intimate relations, or a limitation on their desirable form. Aiming to institutionalize respect (as well as other emotions, such as trust and care) is the muddled result of a process of double translation. First is the translation of the terminology of personal relations into the civic sphere, thus talking about "civic friendship" and "civic respect," and then the translation of the same concepts back into the private and intimate realms, defending "mutual respect" as a mark of intimate relations. This double translation distorts the original meaning of the terminology, and blurs some of the key desirable aspects of both civic and intimate relations. Consequently, terms such as "mutual respect" carry civic expectations that cannot and should not be part of intimate relations.

In other words, respect, trust, and friendship are personal or intimate terms that were transferred to the public realm to describe preferred notions of civic relations. As legal and political theories strive to reconstitute them into the private sphere, they carry with them residues of the public language, which render them inappropriate for the conceptualization of intimate relations. The nonviolence, nondomination, and "egalitarian forms of reciprocity"[28] that Cohen wishes to institute in intimate relations can readily be described as desired forms of civic relations. However, they are not suitable for general application into individuals' intimate lives. This is true not only because they substitute familial harmony (or disharmony) with adversarial self-interested relations (as communitarian critics suspect). The introduction of civic forms of respect into the intimate sphere is undesirable because it sidesteps the multiplicity of acceptable forms of intimate relations, some of which are utterly inappropriate for civic relations. By "acceptable forms of intimate relations," I mean forms that should not be criminalized, directly regulated, or otherwise mandated by the state and its institutions, however unattractive, unproductive, even appalling, they may seem to some outside observers. Society and the state must accept a wide array of preferences and expressions in the intimate domain, much more than in the civic and public sphere where relations and their expression can be regulated more directly through structured paternalist means.

Supporters of the reflexive paradigm thesis could object, inquiring why we should accept those weaknesses of human nature. Why should we not assign institutions such as the criminal law apparatus and law enforcement to direct members of our society toward more productive forms of interaction, more perfect (intimate) unions? Individuals make bad choices in their personal lives, but—the supporter of Cohen's paradigm may continue—it is the responsibility of legal and political theorists to find ways to challenge those mistakes and develop paradigms that would resist and amend them.

Structured paternalism starts from the same assumption, namely, that individuals can make choices that others may regard as flaws or weaknesses. Some of these weaknesses are professed in their intimate lives. It is the state's obligation to provide means for individuals to minimize, or at best prevent, destructive intimate choices when their effects significantly harm one's well-being and ability to fulfill her personal aims, or when they undermine the civic equality of the agent or of those with whom she is intimately connected. Ignoring those weaknesses, in the classical liberal fashion of pushing them into the private unregulated realm, not only undermines the effectiveness of legal and political frameworks; it also hinders the project of justly regulating the relations between the state and its members. On the other hand, institutionalizing a perfectionist response to these weaknesses represents a failure to respect the wide variety of unique choices that individuals make in their intimate lives. Such regulation faults individuals for expressing their identities—sexual, cultural, moral, psychological—in the domain where those identities are not supposed to be negotiated or respected but rather expressed for expression's sake.

Consider the case of domestic violence. The feminist demand to renounce the "this is a private matter" response to instances of domestic violence is entirely defensible. Defending the basic rights of all members is a key commitment of the liberal-democratic state, and the threat to one's life or bodily integrity is a clear violation of rights. Hiding behind privacy claims to oppress, exploit, or harm others is in no way an acceptable use of the right to privacy. However, addressing this formerly private matter mainly (or solely) through the criminal justice system does not answer the moral call, nor the practical demands, that this personal and social problem raises.

Morally speaking, prosecuting a man who abuses his wife can represent a disregard for their separate identities as well as their common lives. Through narrating and analyzing the story of one battered woman, Beth Kyoko Jamieson asserts that the question "Why didn't she leave?" is never a simple one to answer.[29] Women share a lot of the motivation for remaining within abusive relations, because of economic and emotional dependency, concern for other parties involved, love, and other reasons. While these may be preferences adapted to accommodate a bad situation, or a choice of what seems to the woman to be a lesser evil, dismissing her perspective does not always support the restoration of her autonomy or the enhancement of her well-being. Such circumstances cannot productively be explained away through the notion of patriarchy. This does not mean that abused women are to blame for their continued abuse, nor does it mean that they should be deemed autonomous agents and therefore abandoned to bear the consequences of their decision to stay.[30] Contextualizing abuse does not mean excusing it, but rather responding to it more justifiably and more effectively. In many cases of continuous abuse, a sole focus on legal measures against the abusive partner is unlikely to improve the situation. Linda Mills's account of the uselessness of legal responses—including feminist ones—to domestic abuse documents how this tool often fails to help women, men, or society as a whole. According to her, "Whether by virtue of denial, projection, or privilege, mainstream feminists have been able to advocate for a uniform, and ironically conservative, law-and-order response to intimate abuse that blames men and ultimately treats women as innocent victims." This approach is irrelevant to most cases, she claims, and based on her two decades of work in the field of domestic violence, she maintains that "arrest, prosecution, and incarceration do not necessarily reduce the problem of domestic violence and may even be making the problem worse."[31]

Considering more extreme circumstances, take a case that may seem clear-cut at first blush, the case of murder. Taking the life of another person is an act that warrants an intervention by the state's authorities through prosecution and punishment. So sound is the belief in the justifiability of this response that Joseph Raz uses it as a paradigmatic example of intervention that does not hinder autonomous choice (thus distinguishing justifiable forms of paternalism, which do not limit autonomy, from unjustifiable forms). In his discussion of the moral relevance of state coercion, Raz defends the view that "an autonomous life is valuable only to the extent that it is engaged in *valuable* activities and relationships. The loss of an opportunity to murder does nothing to reduce one's chances of having the sort of autonomous life which is of value, hence there is nothing lost in not having the opportunity to murder."[32] Raz suggests that the criminalization of certain choices, choices that are of no value, cannot be regarded as a constraint of autonomy. However, one need not subscribe to a communitarian or relativistic conception of morality to acknowledge that in some traditional cultures, a man's pride and honor—highly valuable cultural assets—are dependent upon "his" women's (wife's and sisters') chastity. Even those who oppose, for moral reasons, such hierarchical gender relations can still recognize that within such a framework, a man could feel obliged to harshly respond to a breach of the codes of acceptable behavior by "his" women. It may be the case that he wishes to punish, even murder, "his" woman if she went astray.

I argue in chapter 5 for measures that the state should take in response to women who are oppressed within their cultural groups. Here the focus is on the responses the state should take toward the perpetrator. The case of murder for "family honor" underlies the argument that the protection of the intimate sphere from crude legal intervention is subsequent to the protection of civic equality and the well-being that generates it; thus, a structured paternalist policy starts with the prevention of destructive choices, ones that often irreversibly limit an individual's opportunities to thrive. Providing appropriate forms of support in the intimate domain, which would protect basic rights such as the right to life, is a first step in the state's justified response to destructive intimate relations. However, even this preliminary step requires an acknowledgment that claims like Raz's that "there is nothing lost" when murder is criminalized are not always accurate. The legal limitations on murder (as well as other, less dramatic choices) can easily be justified under a host of moral and legal conceptions, including that of structured paternalism. But for some, these limitations undermine the possibility to form and exercise their personal and cultural identity. These consequences—understanding the priority of the right to life over family honor in a democracy, for example, or accepting a woman's right to choose her actions—may well be endorsed by anyone who is committed to basic forms of equality (including gender equality). Nonetheless, they represent a (justified) limitation on the development of personal identity within certain cultures. Acknowledging this reduction in the opportunities to lead a fulfilling intimate life is a first step of a proper response by the state.

Murder within the family does not always occur as a result of an attempt to express personal beliefs. More often it is a result of anger, confusion, and other unregulated emotions. The most heartbreaking of those may be the case of infanticide, in which women, often young, often scared, often in denial about their pregnancy, aim to eliminate the results of an unwanted pregnancy by letting their newborns die or by killing them. Commonly, law enforcement's response to such tragic events, when they learn about them, is to prosecute. Again, there are clear social advantages to forbidding all forms of murder and prosecuting perpetrators. But in this case, as in some other cases of tragic intimate choices, structured paternalism can offer responses that are both morally justified and more effective. Safe Haven laws, which allow individuals to drop off newborns they cannot care for, offer a pathway to regulating intimate behaviors around unwanted pregnancies. These laws, which many states passed in the past decade, offer a nondestructive choice where it may have not existed before and provide an institutionally based opportunity that improves the well-being of all involved (relative to their condition before the opportunity existed). Safe Haven laws do not substitute the criminal laws against infanticide; they are an attempt to make them obsolete. Other social mechanisms of support may be needed—for example, additional help for poor women who feel that another baby would jeopardize their ability to provide for their family,[33] the prevention of unwanted pregnancies through educational and other means, and institutional support for families in caring for infants and children. All these amount to a structured paternalist attempt to regulate intimate conduct in the vulnerable context of unwanted pregnancy, through social policies rather than (or in addition to) criminal legal means.

The most difficult challenge for structured paternalism (and other approaches aiming to regulate intimacy) is the need to reconcile the preservation of a sense of intimacy, which defies intervention and endorses a plurality of aims, with the goal of establishing and regulating well-being. Structured paternalism aims to offer pathways to preventing destructive choices that undermine well-being and civic equality while maintaining a broad range of intimate forms of expression that underlie personal well-being.

Justified Regulation of Intimate Choices

The case for intervening in intimate decisions has to be made carefully, because intimate decisions are by definition more significantly value-driven and tied to identity formation than other decisions. A structured paternalist response to intimacy should begin with acknowledging that the first and foremost obligation of the state toward its members in the domain of intimate relations is the prevention of destructive decisions and actions. Avoiding such choices is one of the most basic components of personal well-being, which underlies the development of civic equality. In order to promote equal well-being as a basis for civic equality, the state should expand and structure the scope of acceptable intimate choices, while minimizing the acceptability and probability of destructive choices.

This view is compatible with other approaches such as Darwall's normative welfare approach, Cohen's emphasis on steering self-regulation in the right direction, and Teubner's reflexive paradigm. What the structured paternalism approach to regulating intimacy aims to emphasize, though, is the need to protect the plurality of forms in which identity is constructed and maintained through intimate choices. It accounts for the complex variables that make up intimate decisions, and advocates a policy approach to the intimate sphere that would be more proactive and preventive than punitive. The emphasis is not on desirable outcomes, but on the prevention of the most undesirable outcomes, while leaving as broad a range as possible for individual choice, identity formation, and self-expression. The structured paternalism that is required to accomplish this aim attempts to balance the demands of freedom and respect for a variety of conceptions of the good life on the one hand, with the equal standing of all citizens that demands opportunities to pursue a broad range of goals through a productive set of opportunities on the other hand.

Consequently, deregulation and legal sanctions are less desirable than methods of prevention and the construction of a structured choice set, which extends opportunities for more desirable actions. On the theoretical level, intimacy should be understood as a source of identity and as such receive protection and support. On the policy level, the main avenue for intervention should be the development of structured paternalist interventions to avert potentially destructive intimate choices and behaviors and extend opportunities to pursue other options. Such mechanisms can address intimate matters preventively, rather than responding to them mostly when a breach of law occurs, thus possibly obviating criminal intervention. They allow individuals to manifest various forms of self-regulation, but they do not abandon them in potentially destructive situations, such as unplanned pregnancy or abusive spousal relations. Structured paternalism can and should be sensitive to cultural and personal differences, and thus need not be perfectionist or aim to promote specific outcomes. Rather, it can offer a network of support for individuals in potentially hazardous intimate situations.

Leo Tolstoy's famous observation in *Anna Karenina* that each miserable family is miserable in its own unique way should be recalled here not just for the poetic truth it holds, but also for its relevance for policy making. Universal suggestions that offer recipes for healthy intimate relations (recall Cohen's vision of nondomination and mutual respect in spousal relations) should be treated with great caution. Such caution is warranted in varied cases, from liberal suggestions such as William Galston's to give preference to the two-parent family because of its supposed contribution to children's well-being,[34] to the Bush administration's "marriage initiative," to the ban on adoption by gay couples in some states. Such universal perfectionist claims seem to suggest that we can all be happy if we live up to some institutional ideal of the good or desirable life. The state should refrain from endorsing a given vision, which is overly paternalist and requires levels and forms of intervention that can undermine some identity-related dimensions of intimate relations. Rather, the state should emphasize preventing the most undesirable, destructive outcomes and leave (as well as structure) a broad range of possibilities beyond those destructive ones.

In order to prevent destructive choices in the intimate sphere, unacceptable intimate choices need to be identified. Beyond them, a vast diversity of intimate preferences has to be accepted, allowing for as rich an intimate life as possible to be expressed without social intervention. A choice that should be prevented is one that stands the high risk of being destructive for the individual making it or for other people, usually ones that have intimate relations with her. The long-term, extensive negative potential effects of the decision indicate a wrong intimate decision; often the consequences are irreversible. This type of choice can best be addressed by structuring a better choice set, which offers alternative, more desirable opportunities before the destructive step was taken.

The extension of properly structured choices is more productive in cases that can turn destructive or tragic, as in the case of unwanted pregnancies, or abusive parental or spousal relations. Prevention by offering structured choices is much more productive both from a personal perspective, as it supports the aversion of tragic consequences, and from a public policy perspective, as it can help avert the costs and social consequences of policing and criminal procedures. These structured paternalist measures can also prove helpful in cases that are less dramatic, such as when marital relations go sour.

Taking another look at policies that regulate marriage, it is now possible to argue that it is acceptable under structured paternalism for the state to prefer one form of intimate conduct over another. Thus, it can favor marriage and promote it through tax cuts and other supportive (rather than punitive) means. To make the case for such policy—because it addresses intimate decisions that would not, if taken, be deemed criminal—the state would need to share its justification in the public sphere. Arguing for such policies solely on the basis of religious values, for example, would not suffice. Thus, suggesting that homosexuality is a sin and that same-sex unions should thus be excluded from supports offered to other unions is not an argument based on publicly accessible reasoning. However, if the social facts behind Galston's endorsement of the two-parent family are accurate, it would make sense to express the state's preference for the nuclear family unit through various mechanisms, in particular ones that discourage divorce (and possibly single parenthood by choice). The public debate can accept an argument of the type that Galston offers, because the argument is based on evidence that children do better in two-parent families than they do in single-parent homes. However, this evidence has to be sound enough to merit public support, and disputing claims have to be taken into account. For example, though children from single-parent homes might do poorly by educational and other measures, other factors can significantly contribute to this alleged fact. Single-parent families are much more likely to be poor. Poverty is associated with many risks in children's (and adults') lives, such as educational failure, higher chances of dropping out of school, early and risky sexual behavior, and various health risks. If a marriage initiative of some sort is an attempt to minimize some of these risks, its supporters would do well to consider poverty as a contributing factor to many of these risks, and respond to them through a structured paternalistic response.

The demand to protect or prioritize marriage is often seen as a conservative attempt to impose religious or other traditional values on the public. This short discussion aimed to suggest that it can be argued for and justified by other lines of reasoning, in particular ones that aim at protecting individuals while allowing them the freedom to pursue their personal vision of well-being, both within the intimate sphere and beyond it. Clearly, other initiatives that support certain intimate choices over others through an open public debate can be offered.

The same structured paternalist approach can apply to cases in which cultural differences come into play and sometimes blur the public discussion with less-than-well-argued responses (or what Richard Shweder calls "yuck responses").[35] Take, for example, the well-known case of a group of Seattle doctors, who in 1996 were asked by recent immigrants from Somalia to perform a clitoridectomy on their daughters. Their choice, which in some Western eyes is potentially destructive, was based on their tradition and their personal choice to follow their tradition after they immigrated. The doctors declined to perform the operation, but instead of sending them home with this refusal and with a possible decision to perform the procedure in domestic and less than safe conditions, they looked for an alternative. They suggested soliciting the consent of the girls for performing a minor incision to the clitoral hood, a procedure that could potentially satisfy the demands of the parents, as well as the basic standards of Western medicine and social norms.[36] The public outcry that followed caused the hospital to withdraw the decision, sending the parents and the girls back to the sanctity of the private sphere, to exercise their decisional autonomy with no public intervention, support, or direction. True, paternalism and cultural imperialism were avoided, as well as intervention into the private domain. But without some form of intervention, the chances that the girls suffered more hardship are greater. The risks of traditional clitoridectomy performed at home are much greater than the operation the parents and the hospital could possibly have agreed on. In this case as in others, structured paternalism could have prevented destructive intimate decisions while defining a choice set and supporting individuals in the process of choosing. This form of intervention would take into account the well-being and the range of opportunities of all individuals, adults and children, including their identities and preferences.

Legal intervention in this case is less than helpful. It may not allow for preventive early intervention because of privacy concerns. It further stands at risk of abandoning individuals in vulnerable crossroads to take wrong choices, and suffer the legal and personal consequences. In the case of the Somali immigrants, the solution that the hospital suggested should have been accepted, but the fear of litigation precluded this option. Social institutions other than the criminal legal system can offer structured paternalist mechanisms that would productively respond to such challenges. The welfare system, interdisciplinary ethical boards in hospitals, or advisory boards in family (and other) courts can overcome many of the weaknesses characteristic of the legal systems and paradigms. These structured paternalist policies supplement the protection of basic rights that is provided through the prevention of destructive choices.

As indicated by these examples, many structured paternalist responses would take place outside the legal system; however, some promising work is achieved in the courtroom. In responding to individuals at critical crossroads in their intimate lives, family courts, dependency courts, juvenile courts, and some drug courts establish multidisciplinary teams that evaluate individuals involved and offer recommendations for action. The initiative in some courts offer parents support services including transportation, school and job placement, developmental screenings for infants and toddlers, and even Early Head Start programs. The aim is not punitive but preventive, working toward rehabilitation and encouragement of better intimate (and other, such as employment-related) choices.[37] These individualized approaches can better serve the goal of preventing destructive choices and facilitating the choice of better paths.[38]

A final example where structured paternalism can prove productive is in the management of gang membership. The participation of young teenagers in violent gangs may not seem to some observers to constitute an intimate choice, but the significance of these group relations to identity, affiliation, and intimacy for at least some of the members indicates that these too can sometimes be considered intimate. A structured paternalist approach would focus on offering alternative modes of relating, generating commitment, and offering mutual respect and support outside the confines of a youth gang, and less on punitive measures against gang members. This is not to say that criminal behaviors should be tolerated or explained away because they are possibly part of an individual's intimate choice set. However, a response that focuses on punishing gang members is often ineffective as a solution for gangs and the threats they create; it fails to recognize the important contribution these groups make in the lives of their members, and thus it stands a small chance of changing behavior patterns. By providing alternative opportunities for responding to the same needs and aspirations for which gangs are currently the only route in some neighborhoods, structured paternalism can eliminate many of the destructive choices youngsters make in joining gangs.

I have argued in this chapter that paternalist intervention in the intimate sphere should ideally take the form of extending desirable opportunities and preventing destructive ones. Structured paternalism recognizes that the free expression of preferences in the sphere of intimate relations is critical to the development of identity and subsequently of individual well-being. It thus aims to support the well-being of all individuals through limiting destructive acts that undermine the well-being of vulnerable individuals, while providing all members of society with opportunities to pursue their visions of the intimate good life.

If this argument applies to social policies that relate to adults, how should it be implemented in social policies that address children, who are commonly given fewer opportunities, choices, and decision-making powers? Applying the argument for structured paternalism to the relations of adults with children requires some reconsideration both of the argument itself, and of some common perceptions of the just relations between adults and children in society. In the next chapter, I take a closer look at the relations between adults and children in the context of adult society's obligation to protect children. The challenge of regulating adults' relations with children encapsulates the complexity of allowing intimacy and identity to evolve while minimizing the probability of destructive choices. In this domain as well, it is important to find ways of directing personal choices without sterilizing the forms of expression available to individuals of all ages.

4

PATERNALISM TOWARD CHILDREN

Structured paternalism allows the state to prevent tragic choices and to support the expansion of opportunities individuals have that allow them to pursue their well-being in social and intimate contexts. It is reasonable for the state to develop policies that would treat individuals paternalistically, first, because it is unavoidably a part of the state's function, and second because it stands to support social as well as personal goals, including well-being and civic equality.

What are the consequences of this argument for children? Children seem inherently subject to paternalism, to being directed toward what is deemed by adults to be a better path, to have others decide for them. Primarily paternalism toward children tends to be justified in terms of their limitations and need for protection: children are incapable of figuring out and realizing their long-term interests, and therefore the adults' role—their right, or possibly their duty— is to see that children's choices do not undermine their inferred needs and interests.

In previous chapters, I offered an argument for structured paternalism toward adults, suggesting that making policies with another's well-being in mind is a justified form of social policy making. How does this argument get translated to the realm of adults' institutional relations with children? I focus here mostly on organized relations, because personal relations both within the family and beyond it—as in the relations of a teacher with her young students—require a different set of considerations. Personal relations generally are more permissive about making decisions with the other party's well-being in mind. Self-interest and other calculations are not necessarily the sole approach even for rational choice theorists when they discuss familial and other personal forms of decisions about conduct or expenditures. Hence, this chapter's main focus is on institutional relations between adults and children, the regulation of which is a concern for policy makers on various levels, and which affect groups of children in society rather than being directed toward individual children in a family or a classroom.

Protection is a key organizing concept of adults' relations to children within an institutional context. Legally speaking, children in the Western world are protected by a vast array of rights. Those are aimed at ensuring that children are provided with food, shelter, and education, and that they are spared from violence and neglect. Legal and political theorists strive at expanding the scope of children's rights to cover further areas of their lives. This effort is misguided in the context of the treatment of children in society for the same reasons that it is misguided in the context of regulating intimate relations. The protection of children and childhood requires instituting adults' obligations rather than broadening children's rights, and these obligations can be expressed productively through structured paternalism. In continuation of the argument on providing the conditions for well-being through social policies that allow intervention and regulation, I argue that similar to adults, children need and deserve active support to thrive. The rights framework does not provide such active support, beyond the basic set, which should be maintained. As we have seen in the previous chapter, the conceptual framework of the right to privacy, while important, fails to deliver its promise to all members of the family and to ensure that they can pursue their goals. Similarly, children's rights provide a crucial foundation for protection. However, they do not offer sufficient protection, guidance, and support for children within the family and beyond.

Society should therefore prefer structured forms of paternalism and derive from this approach specific institutional obligations, including obligations on the part of adults in the family, the welfare system and medical institutions, and the education system. In the context of treating children, structured paternalism takes a more protective form in that it assumes more vulnerability on the part of its recipients. Protective paternalism is valuable for supporting children's developmental needs and shielding them from destructive decisions that they and others might make. In addition, protective paternalism recognizes children's current state and emphasizes present-time needs and preferences of the stakeholders (children and the adults in their lives). Contrary to the common future orientation of theoretical and social approaches, which have a tendency to focus on the just and efficient ways of turning children into specific types of adults (most commonly citizens),[1] I defend a view of children and childhood as deserving an equal social standing to adulthood. This approach is based on regarding childhood not as an impediment but rather as the first of many steps that together make up human life. Structured paternalist policies are thus developed in this chapter to complement basic rights protection as an appropriate way for adult society to respond to children.

Children's Rights and Their Limits

At the beginning of the twentieth century, Ellen Key pronounced it "the Century of the Child";[2] less than a century later, Neil Postman lamented "the Disappearance of Childhood."[3] The Century of the Child became possible through legislation establishing various rights, which facilitated the emergence of the contemporary Western conception of childhood. Many societies outside today's Western world do not share its current conception of childhood,[4] which is based on describing children as different from adults in terms of their respective abilities to participate in economic exchanges and sexual relations[5] in ways that promote their well-being.

Childhood, as the Western world understands it today, evolved through the endorsement of laws and treaties protecting children from physical abuse, neglect, work at a young age, premature marriage, and other previously unquestioned social practices. Past and present societies expect young people to join the struggle to support the family at very early ages, in the field, factory, or sweatshop. Only when consistent and reliable protection is ensured can real childhood evolve from mere young age. While significant differences have been traced among parents of different social classes, the key notions of protection permeated developed countries' notions of parenting.[6] Western cultures aim to ensure the protection of children by endowing them with rights, hence manifesting their social standing as persons rather than semi-persons, their parents' property, or extensions of their parents. Still, they are viewed as inhabiting a unique space that demands special considerations.

Legislation that defines and protects children stems from an acknowledgment of traits that society recognizes as unique to youth and which it wishes to promote. The "open future,"[7] "promise,"[8] and "innocence"[9] are all terms used nowadays to characterize children, that is, young persons who are relieved of the struggle for survival. Some of the more romantic aspects of these contemporary conceptions of childhood date back to Jean-Jacques Rousseau and his vision of the natural child.[10] Childhood emerges when young persons' responsibility to self-protection is taken over by adults, including the state, which uses its powers to recognize, shape, and respond to what it perceives as the fundamental traits of children. Whenever the personal struggle for survival prevails—in the form of threats to one's life or strife of breadwinning or rearing one's own children—childhood disappears.

However, even those who enjoy the more privileged circumstances of cultural norms and legislation that allow them to live as children in their early years are rapidly losing their childhood. Traits such as curiosity, optimism, and a sense of open paths have been protected in Western countries since the early twentieth century through keeping children as far as possible outside the adult world of parenthood, economic worries, and violence. In our time, the walls shielding children's lives from what they supposedly cannot contain are cracked again.[11] Children are admitted—or pulled—into the adult world through exposure to sex and violence in the media, as well as through the cultural conception of everyone, including young persons, as responsible for their own choices. "Children are no longer protected, but are prepared for a harsh, over-sophisticated adult existence"[12] at an early age. In these and other ways, children share some of the dimensions of adult life.

Furthermore, some theoretical trends advocate expanding the range of children's rights in an effort to abolish paternalism and to offer children an equal standing in society. Child liberationists argue that children should have the same rights of self-determination as adults.[13] Thus, they implicitly endorse choice-protecting rights for children, an approach that is justifiably criticized in the literature.[14] Child liberation and child-centered education, two trends that were at their peak in the 1960s and 1970s, construe children's rights as similar to those of adults. Advocates of free education, such as A. S. Neill and Carl Rogers, made an impressive effort to implement the idea of equality and liberty for children in educational institutions.[15] But such liberty is often an additional burden cast over children's shoulders, turning them into small adults, their newly won childhood fading away.

A small number of authors have questioned in recent years the validity of rights conceptions as a tool for protecting the well-being of children.[16] Onora O'Neill argues for imperfect obligations—ones not accompanied by corresponding rights—as fundamental to the appropriate treatment of children.[17] James Dwyer calls for a child-centered conversation about children—one that takes into account their perspectives.[18] And Barbara Arneil suggests that care ethics, based on Carol Gilligan's psychological theory as well as on communitarian understandings of society, should replace strict notions of rights and justice in the conceptualization of children's place in society.[19]

What these approaches point to is that beyond securing children's basic rights, democratic societies need to clearly define the obligations adults have toward them. Respect and protection are the two major values that lie at the heart of structured paternalism toward children. Structured paternalist policies can best be practiced in established social institutions, fulfilling adults' obligations toward children. These obligations are much more limited than what David Archard calls "the caretaker thesis," which is usually defended "within the context of liberal political philosophical presuppositions about autonomy and paternalism."[20] They are less comprehensive than the liberal demand to coerce a child into a future of autonomy and rationality. They are even thinner than Joel Feinberg's argument for a "right to an open future." I assume that adults' obligations toward children are not derivative of the latter's supposed innate incapability to reason or efficiently practice a right to self-determination. Adults' obligations toward children are derived from two sources: first, from the acknowledgment of children as deserving the basic rights ascribed to them in Western theory and social practices, including respect of their agency; and second, from children's greater physical, emotional, and economic vulnerability and dependence.

Rights are the first layer of protection, enabling young people to exist as children, while obligations are the second layer of protection, compatible with the first.[21] The institution of adults' obligations encourages the implementation of the protection embedded in the language of rights, while putting the responsibility for children's lives and well-being in the hands of adults, who are to design corresponding policies that protect and enhance children's well-being.

I share with other critics of rights the acceptance (which is often suggested only implicitly) of paternalism as a dimension of the justified way for adult society to relate to children. Expanding children's rights may distort the social conceptualization of childhood and result in a focus on their decisional autonomy, which is far less necessary or justified than the protection of their well-being, including by use of paternalist means. Children's inherent vulnerability necessitates a stronger way of protecting them, without impairing their present and future ability to choose and to thrive, and while keeping in mind their current well-being and future civic equality. Establishing adults' obligations as the moral component responsive to children's vulnerability is more productive both morally and politically than endowing more rights to children. These obligations can be fulfilled through paternalist social institutions and processes, in ways that are linked to structured paternalism toward adults. In other words, these processes will be motivated by children's inferred needs and interests, and they would express respect and strive for well-being and future civic equality through the expansion of opportunities.

How are the forms of paternalism toward the two age groups to be distinguished? "Whether to regard children as pure, bestial, innocent, corrupt, charged with potential, *tabula rasa,* or even as we view our adult selves"[22] is a choice dependent on time, culture, and inclination. The delineation of childhood from adulthood needs to be conceptualized with a goal in mind; the understanding offered for what these periods of human life mean should be based on the reasoning for the question, on what the distinction is aimed to achieve. In the medical professions, the division between general and pediatric medicine is undertaken because children are relevantly different from adults in their sensitivity to certain illnesses, the structure and function of some of their organs, and thus the medical treatment they need. Why should democratic theory distinguish adults from children when focusing on issues of paternalism and choice?

First, as mentioned earlier, democratic theory in general needs a distinction between these two groups for the purpose of efficiency. The allocation of certain rights, including political rights, needs to rest on some structural differentiation. Beyond the allocation of political rights and certain regulated behaviors (such as driving), the distinction between children and adults in the specific context of paternalism and choice is required in order to justify different forms of social protection allotted to the two groups. The need to distinguish adults from children is necessitated by the different choice sets and opportunities the two groups can benefit from, relative to their respective capacities, vulnerabilities, and interests.

As indicated in chapter 2, many theorists distinguish adults from children in order to justify differentiated forms of intervention in personal decision making. These theorists oppose paternalism as demeaning, arguing that it befits children and therefore is unsuitable, and offensive, for adults. Understanding the relevant distinctive factors between the two groups as well as their similarities can support a sounder argument regarding the use of paternalism in social policies. In what follows, I consider the unique features of childhood along with the dimensions it shares with adulthood in order to advance the argument that structured paternalism is a reasonable approach to social policies relating, albeit differently, to the two groups.

The vulnerability of children's lives and the dependence of their well-being on adults create immanent inequality between children and adults. The recognition of children as rights bearers and the institution of basic rights for children proved to be helpful in supporting children's well-being. However, this recognition creates the risk of obscuring children's vulnerability and erroneously characterizing them as fully capable of independent decision making and self-guidance. In the next section, I consider an equal social standing for childhood and respect for children as a substitute for further rights. Respectful forms of paternalism are suggested as an appropriate way of responding to children's vulnerabilities and addressing their needs.

Beyond Future Adults: Paternalism across Ages

Children and adults can be differentiated by their physical traits, such as size, sensitivity to illnesses, and motor skills. They can be told apart by some of their conceptions about the world, such as "magical thought" and distinctive conceptions of time[23]—aspects that should be considered in constituting just policies. Other parameters, especially those that bear moral significance, are mostly statistical, a matter of measure rather than of essence. Most children have less knowledge than most adults in the same social circumstances. They are rarely economically independent, and they are less capable of taking into account multiple considerations when making decisions.[24] Even within an argument such as Locke's, which is based on reason as the differentiating feature of human adults from other beings, the gradual nature of the distinction is recognized. Locke maintains that reason is available to children as early as they understand language and suggests that if children experience favorable conditions, reason slowly develops into rationality.[25] The gradual formation of reason does not allot children with full civic equality, though. As Locke famously stated, "Children, I confess, are not born in this full state of equality, though they are born to it."[26] Through this line of reasoning, children are viewed as deficient in comparison to adults, and thus they must await their equal standing in society. Adults are presumed rational and thus independent and autonomous; children are to be socialized until they reach this state.

A common practice in liberal theory is to consider childhood as a passing phase and regard children mostly as the adults they will—or should—become. In Rousseau's words, "We know nothing of childhood, and with our mistaken notions the further we advance the further we go astray. The wisest writers . . . are always looking for the man in the child without considering what he is before he becomes a man."[27] Rousseau's romantic vision of the natural child aside, there is strength to his claim that children should be viewed by adult society not merely as what they are to become, but also for what, and who, they are.

There is no specific point in the process of development that turns children into adults. Realizing the flexibility of the concept of childhood and its contextuality should lead to abandoning the dichotomous view of "childhood" and "adulthood" in a variety of contexts, and specifically in the context of affording choice and structuring justified paternalist policies. Such a dichotomous view usually serves as a silent assumption in theoretical discussions of children as subordinate to adults' perspectives, particularly as those perspectives pertain to the desirable future of their family, community, and society. Most of the theoretical discussions of childhood in educational and political theory tend to regard childhood not only as clearly distinct from adulthood but also as inferior to it. This depiction of childhood and of children is the backdrop of the suggestion that paternalism is good for children, but not for adults: if children are inferior to adults, it makes sense for adults to treat them as such, while expecting a different treatment for themselves.

Treating children paternalistically makes sense within this common conceptual framework because it portrays childhood as a passage toward adulthood, which is considered the more complete state of human existence. Ranging from theories focused on democratic and civic education to pluralist and conservative theories, authors commonly regard society's future as the basis of adults' social relations with children, and consequently as the main aim of the growth process, usually minimizing the importance of the process itself to the lives of those undergoing it, thus minimizing, or failing to acknowledge and respect, children's agency. Giving children the opportunity to choose their own path thus makes little sense, because they cannot make reasonable or justified choices; moreover, their choices could undermine their own well-being in the future, as well as the future of their family, community, or nation, and therefore may be counterproductive to their own interests (as they would understand them if they were rational agents). Minimizing their choice sets, and deciding for them, is thus reasonable within this framework.

Very few theorists challenge this hidden set of priorities.[28] In her critical discussion of liberal perspectives on children, Arneil notes that "[a]n important aspect of viewing children from the perspective of the citizens they are about to become is that they are defined in terms of what they lack."[29] This approach is clearly presented in

Kantian theory, which provides the underpinning for liberal theories today. Theorizing childhood with the kingdom of ends in mind, although it is not a binding value even for Kantians,[30] entails a concentration on specific human attributes. These are described by Kantians as attributes characterizing adults.[31] The Kantian conception of humanity as based on rationality and autonomy leads to a focus on the shortcomings of childhood as its most prominent characteristics. Working within the Kantian framework necessitates giving precedence to (a Kantian form of) rationality, autonomy, and morality. Within this framework, children are examined in light of their (in)capacity, or mere potential, to exhibit these traits.

But the focus on rationality and autonomy, which is suggested by Kantian scholars as a differentiating factor between adults and children, justifying the normative superiority of adults, can in fact expose similarities of human experience at different ages and developmental stages. Understanding the comparability of children and adults along these traits can in turn serve to justify a more careful differentiation between these two social groups.

Developmental psychology has described the emergence of autonomy in children and noted the gradual process of acquiring this trait.[32] Considering the process of developing autonomy along a spectrum (rather than a dichotomy of autonomous capacity), it seems reasonable to assume a qualitative difference between young children, perhaps below the age of seven, and others. Still, the passing of time alone offers only a limited guarantee to the evolvement of autonomy. The earlier stages of human life are essentially characterized by a striking imbalance between profound dependence on the goodwill of others and a minute, slowly growing self-dependence or autonomy. Infants are clearly not autonomous, in that they cannot form complex wishes or communicate preferences effectively. At two years of age, children will normally rebel against external demands and try to establish their own small but significant territory of autonomous decision making (even if its major content may be when not to take a bath). As they grow, their demands for autonomy will increase, along with their capacity to exercise their judgment and their need for advice and guidance. There is no given point in time when the inescapable fact of the newborn's dependence on adults' goodwill vanishes, to be replaced by autonomy and self-authorship. The universal human phenomenon of an ever-changing balance between autonomy and dependence is the basis of the suggestion that there is no clear dichotomy between children and adults in those traits that are relevant for defining moral or social status and thus for justifying paternalism toward them.

Despite the suggestion that children and adults cannot be dichotomously distinguished from each other on the basis of key traits, some policies justifiably demand an artificial dividing line in order to allocate various duties and rights, such as voting rights. Democratic states need to decide who is eligible to participate in electing representatives to the governing bodies; for such purposes, defining eligibility by declaring the eighteenth birthday (or some other age) as the exact point of passage into adulthood is practically and politically plausible. Telling apart those who are eligible, because they are assumed to be capable of benefitting from these rights and contributing to society through them, from those who are not (yet) is a practical necessity. There are other practical (mainly legal) justifications to designating a certain age as appropriate for acquiring a driver's license, as the age of sexual consent, or as the age of legal responsibility. All of these somewhat arbitrary judgments are based on statistical assumptions about the capability of people of a specific age to drive carefully, decide autonomously on their sexual conduct, or be sufficiently morally developed. Considering every person individually to see if they have reached the threshold of autonomy would invade their privacy too severely, not to mention that the cost of such policy could be prohibitive.

The somewhat arbitrary distinction between age groups is required also for the structural purposes of the education system. Mandatory, state-sponsored education is dependent upon a clear definition of eligibility, and therefore children are defined by their age as the recipients of education. I argue later on for certain forms of state-sponsored adult education, but those would not be mandatory. However, while the formal education system is justified to paternalistically restrict children's freedom of choice through mandatory education and other regulations, the relations between adults and children within this system need not be founded on the assumption of a distinct, hierarchical differentiation between children and adults. While children's growth is an unavoidable conceptual as well as empirical fact, it must not be the focal point of their moral relations with adults, in society in general, and particularly in the education system. Hence, it might be necessary for social purposes to define the recipients of mandatory education in terms of age; but it by no means requires describing them to be in a state of want, or as in need of being raised in a certain way whether they like it or not[33] and structuring the curriculum around their deficiencies vis-à-vis their future roles. The educational relations of adults to children, as manifest in the choices of pedagogy and curriculum, need not rely on a strict hierarchical distinction between the two groups, even when the structure of the institution does rely on this hierarchy.

For the purpose of delineating and arguing for just policies, including paternalist ones that are addressed toward children, childhood should not be distinguished from adulthood through its definition as a passing phase of impaired maturity. Neither should it be depicted as indistinguishable from adulthood, as some children's rights advocates construe it in their attempt to equalize the status of children. Rather, it should be recognized as a unique yet equally significant part of human development, worthy of respect and consideration, as well as protection. To use Barbara Arneil's terms, children should be viewed as "being" rather than as "becoming."[34] Childhood is not to be perceived as an impediment or as a passage toward another world—the world of adulthood. As such, it has its own characteristics, which should be regarded not as deficiencies—in relation to adulthood—but rather as qualities relevant to this stage of life, some of which tend to dissolve or evolve into other traits as time passes.

As long as children are not morally blameworthy as a group, the essence of adults' relations with them cannot be the attempt to change them. This may seem like a fundamental rejection of education within the family as well as in the formal education system, but in fact it is the basis for a much more modest claim. Respect for children requires constituting their relations with adults on the recognition of their vulnerability as well as the value of this stage of life, equivalent to the value of other life stages. As such, the process of education, although recognizing and supporting the inevitable change that is part of childhood—and of any other stage in human life—should focus more on the present rather than on the future, hence respecting children for who they are now.

In practice, this kind of respect would require that the education system and other institutions treat children with forms of paternalism that are justified for adults, even if the structure of specific paternalist policies may need to be tailored to children's circumstances. This approach would require offering children choice sets that would make sense to them and would lead them to make productive choices. Compulsory education laws are justified within this approach because they offer a way to avoid irreversible destructive decisions, such as preferring eternal summer vacation over the development of skills and knowledge. This is a default rule that can be breached only with the significant support of family and with the provision of alternative modes of development (such as homeschooling).

While education can be mandated, the goal of developing capacities should be taking into account children's current preferences. Giving children choice within the schooling process, and taking into account their individual priorities to the extent possible within this large system, is a way to express respect while maintaining reasonable levels of paternalist intervention. This form of choice, provided to children within the institutions they inhabit and through a carefully crafted setting is important, independent of the opportunity given to their families to choose which institution they attend.[35]

The argument here, as in previous chapters, that childhood and adulthood should be conceptualized as a spectrum rather than a dichotomy for the purpose of making structured paternalist policies is made in relation to all ages, starting from the very beginning of life. Infants are to a large extent ignored in current conceptualizations of human society.[36] Infancy can be treated respectfully within the forms of the stricter paternalism it elicits, which results from the necessity to interpret and infer the preferences and needs of infants.

Romantic philosophers and educators, like Rousseau and even more so A. S. Neill, suggest that we are morally required to respect the baby's request for food and movement, rather than limiting them—as was common in both authors' times—to feeding by the clock or restraining their hands to avoid thumb sucking. Both authors justify this claim by moral reasoning, as well as by claiming that free, natural education is more effective for raising moral and content adults. Few contemporary authors have taken up the difficult topic of respect for infants and its consequences for moral relations within society.[37] Respecting an infant's needs, without abandoning the responsibility and discretion that is inherent to the institution and execution of structured paternalist policies, is a first step toward respecting and safeguarding childhood, and adulthood. This first step is built on the recognition that persons of all ages strive to achieve balance between areas of dependence and independence in their lives.[38]

So far, the argument has been aimed at establishing a basic comparison between adults and children, suggesting that the relative congruence between these two groups requires significant comparability in the way their interests and needs are conceptualized and addressed through social policies. However, beyond this general claim that grounds policies toward children—including structured paternalist policies—on a respectful foundation, children have unique traits that must be considered by public institutions when designing policies tailored for children's needs. The challenge of preserving equal respect while acknowledging difference is not unique to adult-child relations. Social relations between the genders, as well as those between mainstream ethnic groups and immigrants and minorities, pose similar challenges, which are explored in the next section.

Paternalism and Deviation from the Norm

The common justification of paternalism toward children, as stated, is based on their perceived deficiencies when they are compared to adults, who serve as the social norm. In this sense, children's social status is comparable to the status women held for many centuries.[39] The differences in physical, social, and political vulnerability between children and adults, like those between women and men, result from a combination of biological and socially constructed factors. However, the different factors play a different role in the two sets of groups. Subsequently, the appropriate democratic response to women's social weaknesses is often to abolish them or to reconstitute them as acceptable differences; children's vulnerabilities, on the other hand, need to be accepted, respected, and protected through relevant paternalist social policies.

The suggestion that paternalism is appropriate toward both adults and children, albeit in different ways, goes against some common views in democratic theory. In her Kantian discussion, Tamar Schapiro probes the question "What is a child, such as it would be appropriate to treat a person like one?" Her answer is based on a directive form of paternalism that she regards as essential to adult-child relations: "In 'treating someone like a child' I mean interacting with her on the basis of more paternalistic standards than those which apply to adult-adult relations."[40] Directive paternalism, or taking decisions in spite of the other's will and for (what is interpreted as) her own good, is indeed an unavoidable part of adult-child relationships, at least at younger ages. But in using directive paternalism as the defining, distinguishing quality of adult-child relations, Schapiro conceptualizes children as clearly distinguishable from adults in their capacities. In so doing, she regards children's subservience to adults' will as given, morally acceptable, and even productive. But if lack of knowledge, weakness of will, and irrational inclinations are more prevalent among children while also common in adult behavior, directive paternalism can be formulated to complement protective paternalism as it applies in different times to all members of society. In other words, adults, like children, can use direction and protection at various stages of their lives, and thus paternalist policies that delineate choice sets, establish default rules, and limit destructive choices are applicable to individuals of all ages at certain points in their lives. While treating children in directive paternalist ways would sometimes be justified—deferring their will to that of their parents or others—the definitive approach to regulating children's behavior in private and most significantly in public contexts would be that of protective paternalism, or the supportive intervention that stems from a commitment to their well-being. In this sense, and counter to Kantian and other liberal and democratic arguments, paternalism will not be the distinguishing features of policies and actions directed toward children.

Children's unfamiliarity with some general facts and norms should be understood as further aspects of childhood vulnerability that render them dependent on adults' goodwill. These inherent features of youth can better be understood when considered in relation to the case of an immigrant in a foreign country, with language, culture, and traditions that are unfamiliar to her.[41] Being a stranger in a strange land offers a partial opportunity to recall what it means to be a child in an adult world. At first, one may not understand the language. For a long time after mustering the words, communicating her exact thoughts and meanings may still be difficult for the immigrant. Often she might miss social cues and fail to realize common wisdom and practices. As Schapiro claims, "An adult who laughs at your bald spot is to be resented; a child who does the same is to be disciplined."[42] But neither of these assumptions is necessarily correct. An adult may not be aware of the expectations and sensitivities of your culture; he may come from a culture where mockery can be a way of breaking tensions or expressing close friendship. Resentment would be out of place in such circumstances. It would be more just to refer to such differences as vulnerabilities on the side of the newcomer, and to respond accordingly. It is hard to blame an adult who fails to follow social rules she is not familiar with, and resenting her for misconduct could be a sign of ethnocentricity (or xenophobia) rather than a sign of respect for her autonomy, of treating her as an adult.

A child who expresses herself in socially objectionable ways should be disciplined, claims Schapiro. But disciplining on such occasions can reflect two unfounded assumptions. First, it assumes that the child already knows how to behave in this context, for example, understanding that comments on hair style (or lack thereof) can be offensive. The child's failure to follow the rules is assumed to merit punishment. Second, it positions the child as an object for the adult to reshape, rather than seeing her as a subject, or agent, who can learn social norms by participating in social relations and processes. There is little point in punishing or disciplining the child who did not behave according to a social code she did not internalize yet, unless one believes that punishment is a proper form of socialization, or a helpful way to introduce children to social expectations. It makes more sense to repeatedly introduce her to the social code as an expression of the respect she deserves as someone who is still learning the rules—an inherent characteristic of childhood.[43]

The consequences of this form of protective paternalism toward adults were discussed in previous chapters. As for adult-child relations, protective paternalism can lead adults to protect children from what they cannot handle, and from what endangers them as individuals and as a group. This weaker form of paternalism—protective rather than directive—can shield children from various violations of their interests and well-being, while allowing them to grow at their own pace. As with the introduction of social norms about behavior, which is most likely to take place in relational (familial or educational) contexts, social policies should focus on children as agents and support their introduction into society while respecting their views and current states.

Thinking of children as newcomers to society can further highlight the spectrum of dependence, vulnerability, and subsequent justified paternalism that can be manifest in various circumstances and periods throughout one's life. This framework further draws attention to inaccurate conceptualizations that arise from describing one group (men, adults, native citizens) as the norm in a society, and from the expectation that others not deviate from this norm. It can also address the incompatibility of policies designed with this group of normative members in mind to a diverse society where individuals of various genders, ages, and origins are all equal members. These facts of pluralism can thus be accommodated within a system of protective structured paternalism when it accounts for the requirement to equally respect the needs and preferences of members of all groups in a just, democratic society.

Respecting Vulnerability: Paternalism toward Children

The ways in which adult society perceives and interprets children's unique traits turn them into either advantageous or disempowering qualities. Children's flexibility, their lack of knowledge and abilities, their dependence and other characteristics can—if respected and protected—allow them to try different directions, develop their identities open-mindedly, and discover their own paths as they grow. In other settings, if they are regarded as deficiencies, these very traits can disempower children, close their minds, and limit their sense of confidence in themselves and in others. In more extreme (though still widespread) circumstances, children's traits can endanger their well-being as well as their lives, when taken advantage of by malicious or closed-minded adults. Structured paternalism, and the protective implementation of adults' understanding of children's needs, can provide a framework for society to design respectful policies for them.

The direct dependence of young people's well-being on the way they are perceived and treated by adults provides the basis for adults' moral obligation to protect children. It is in the hands of adults—it is their obligation—to interpret children's characteristics in ways that are conducive rather than limiting, and to protect children in the first steps of their lifelong mission of discovering and choosing their ways of life. For children to be able to accomplish that mission, appropriate defaults should be set for their social development, and well-structured choice sets are to be offered to children and families. Policies that support a family's ability to provide for its children and to treat them well are also part of the same framework, as suggested earlier in the discussion of the intimate sphere. Another appropriate default is compulsory education. In the next chapter, the argument is extended to justify protection for a broad range of cultural practices within the family and community.

The moral consequence of acknowledging children's vulnerability is thus not a carte blanche for paternalism or for decision making on behalf of children; rather, it is a continuation of the structured paternalist social policies, extended and adapted to the context of childhood. Paternalism in this context should express the commitment of adult society and its institutions to organize children's available paths in a way that acknowledges their vulnerabilities and the obligations they generate.

The allocation of these obligations should be divided between the family and public institutions. Adult family members—parents or guardians, and other adults who are in an intimate relation with the child—hold a primary obligation to look after the child's health, her development, and her general well-being, and to protect her from physical danger and exploitation. Some authors defend a precedence of parents' duties and obligations over those of other institutions.[44] But taking for granted any parent's natural goodwill for her child as well as her innate capacity to act upon her good intentions is not justified. Social policies should take into account the potential for intimate destructive choices and prevent them to the extent possible. Parental paternalism exists within the family in various forms and to varying degrees; policies expressing structured paternalism will encompass both children and adult members of the family to offer direction and protection by structuring institutional responses to their preferences and needs. In this way, the fulfillment of adults' obligations toward children is shared by the family and social institutions, including the education, health care, and legal systems. Public institutions bear a greater obligation for protecting children's rights, as rights have little room or meaning in the intimate sphere of the family. (An infringement of children's rights within the family is possible, of course, as in the case of abuse; social institutions need to step in and protect the children. Absent such infringements, there is not much room to express rights in intimate contexts.) By allowing children to play an increasing decisional part in controlling their lives as they grow and develop, through expanding their choice sets and offering them further opportunities to choose, obligation-based, protective paternalism toward children evolves into the general form of structured paternalism. This process requires making an effort to reveal children's needs and listen to their expressed interests. Public institutions must be attuned to children's personal and communal voices and express respect for their perspectives by incorporating them into social policies. Thus, the health care system is responsible for the protection of children from endangering or impeding decisions, such as those made on their behalf by parents and other individuals from cultures that ban lifesaving treatment for children. The medical community's obligation is to find ways of reconciling those cultural traditions or individual standpoints with the protection of the children concerned, and to represent the children's interests when they conflict with those of their guardians.[45] The welfare system and the legal system also carry obligations to protect children, to represent their interests, and to contribute to their present well-being (and consequently to their future opportunities).

The education system is the social institution that probably carries most of the weight of reflecting this view of paternalism, as most children spend significant parts of their childhood under its control. In correlation to child-centered approaches, structured paternalism toward children requires focus on children's present perspectives.[46] Neglecting the present perspectives of children is not only disrespectful and not only results in an unjust and myopic society; it also expresses a deep disregard for childhood itself. The very notion of time and its conceptualization by children (as Jean Piaget noted) render the future largely unimaginable for them. Taking into account children's conception of time requires respecting children's present rather than focusing mainly on preparing them for a future they can hardly grasp.

The fulfillment of adults' obligations in schools, as in other public institutions, should take the form of structured protective paternalism—it should not only take into account the expressed views of children whenever possible, but should also carefully interpret their interests. This interpretation should be designed openly, so as to allow for the child herself to amend it according to her own perspective as she grows. These obligations can best be expressed by structured paternalist approaches—ones that begin with a limited choice set and expand to incorporate further aspects of children's interests, and offer them further opportunities for developing and expressing their preferences.

Conclusion

Social policies that are directed toward children should be built on a respectful consideration of what characterizes this period of life, and should evade the use of adult perspectives and abilities as a social standard. Like other aspects of diversity, age, including young age, should be regarded with respect. Society's approach to children and childhood should not be based on the attempt to adapt what is unique about youth to the standards of adult society.

Since dependence is what fundamentally characterizes childhood, adult society should protect this vulnerable stage of life without losing sight of the respect it entails. The appropriate perspective on children's dependence is one that respects and protects it, while acknowledging that dependence and the need for social respect and protection characterize individuals of all ages. Paternalism toward children should thus be structured on the same scale as other forms of paternalism in society, while considering the varying capacities and needs of children in the construction of specific policies.

To express the vision of equal respect for children, social policies should refrain from implementing paternalist policies based on age distinctions alone. Paternalism in its proper form can be justified for both adults and children because it is not demeaning to either. Rather, it is a tool that can support individuals across the age spectrum in expanding their opportunities and allowing them to exercise their freedom. The personal well-being of both adults and children can be enhanced by a greater focus on the part of policy makers on constructing choice sets that would be good for them.

The expectation that children will "get over" their childhood, while empirically grounded, does not provide a sound basis to adults' relations with children. It risks treating youth as a corridor toward true human existence—adulthood—rather than as an equal, immanent part of life. Society should learn to allow children to experience and enjoy their youth, and protect them from what they cannot contain, decide, or be responsible for. A child is only beginning the gradual, lifelong process of knowing her abilities and desires; thus, she should not be made responsible for long-term choices and their consequences. She should be supported, often more than adults, in the process of learning to discover, define, and express her preferences. If children are protected from what they cannot handle and are enabled to benefit from relevant, appropriate opportunities, the obligations of adults toward them will be closer to being fulfilled.

—ɯ— **5** —ɯ—

Exit with Caution

On Culture and Choice

Liberalism has a contentious relation to culture. Liberal scholars, including those committed to cultural rights, often eye cultural groups with suspicion as they consider granting them group rights, intervening in their practices, or protecting their vulnerable members. It seems that many liberal theories are concerned with minimizing the damage that culture does to individuals or to society, sometimes proposing ways to curb the harmful effects of culture on individual flourishing or on political equality. The vision of society upon which many liberal theories rest is one in which there is a "general" or mainstream society, where liberal principles of autonomy, individuality, and rationality reign, and within which enclaves of encompassing groups endorse practices that compromise some of these core principles of mainstream society. For this line of liberal thinking, one major challenge is how to respond to individuals within illiberal subgroups, some of whom may be perfectly content with their condition (albeit not necessarily in a reflective way), while others may be oppressed or wish to leave for other reasons. Most liberal responses to the challenge presented by illiberal culture share a common feature: support for exit rights. As Susan Okin puts it, "Any consistent defense of group rights or exemptions that is based on liberal premises has to ensure

89

that at least one individual right—the right to exit one's group of origin—trumps any group right. . . . Not to be able to leave the group in which one has been raised for an alternative mode of life is a serious violation of the kind of freedom that is basic to liberalism."[1]

This view is representative of the vision examined critically throughout this book, namely, that choice is more desirable than social intervention, and that the state must offer all members an opportunity to freely express their preferences through their actions rather than organize, limit, or structure their choices. In this chapter, I challenge exit rights in the context of this vision of the relations between individual and state. I argue that in their minimalist form, exit rights do not amount to much more than lip service, stating that all must be able to exit but providing little detail about how this exit is to be realized, let alone support for its realization. In their more substantial form, exit rights are construed to require interventions that threaten core values of some cultural subgroups, and thus fail to support a true accommodation of cultural differences. I suggest that less interventionist policies, dubbed here entrance paths, should play a substantial role in the democratic response to the challenge of culture and diversity.[2] Those policies and the social structures that accompany them can provide opportunities similar to those of substantial exit rights, without the moral burden that is the consequence of interventions related to exit rights. A look at one institutional response—that of schools—to either exit rights or entrance paths reveals the greater potential of the second for accommodating the needs of members of nonreflective communities in liberal democracies while preserving these communities. In particular, the argument focuses on adults rather than on children as the relevant recipients of these policies, and on support systems within general society rather than on interventions into subcultures.

Thus, this chapter presents a case of applying structured paternalism in a democratic society by organizing personal and communal decisions while maintaining a commitment to freedom and ethical individualism. Freedom is protected in this account through the structured support for expanding opportunities to individuals. The value of self-expression and free identity formation must in this context be balanced with other liberal and democratic values, in light of the ways in which identity is formed within the family and other institutions, particularly schools. Structured paternalism that protects children and expands adults' opportunities is suggested as a way to balance these competing values.

A quick comment on definitions: for the purpose of the current discussion, I follow a fairly noncontroversial description of culture offered in the otherwise provocative work of Bhikhu Parekh: "Culture is a historically created system of meaning and significance or, what comes to the same thing, a system of beliefs and practices, in terms of which a group of human beings understand, regulate and structure their individual and collective lives." [3] Note that I refer to cultural groups as a broad categorization, incorporating both religions and other forms of cultural affiliation; a lot of what I have to say about nonreflective communities is most relevant in the context of traditional religious groups.

Nonreflective Communities in Liberal Democracies

The accommodation of cultural subgroups challenges liberal democracies to closely consider their value systems and their democratic practices. Does liberal democracy offer an open-ended framework within which "anything goes"? Or is it founded on a set of values that all members are expected to endorse? And, if the latter, how can freedom of thought and association be protected? Nonreflective communities, or those that espouse illiberal visions of the good life, further complicate this challenge. A common assumption is that liberal-democratic ideals are threatened by a broad range of nonreflective communities, and that the goals and practices of these communities stand in contrast to those of liberal democracy. How should a liberal-democratic polity respond to illiberal views, including religious ones? Should these views be discouraged, or would such a response undermine the very cause of liberal democracies? And if they are tolerated, would that not create a danger in the form of subgroups within the citizenry that reject, and possibly actively oppose, basic tenets of society? Moreover, how will the rights of individuals within these communities be protected?

These are some of the originating questions of a heated debate within academe, in the judiciary, and in the public sphere. Responses to these questions range from calls for providing institutional support to all cultures, to proposals for Socratic education as a means to developing autonomy in all children.[4] In other words, the responses cover liberal-democratic views ranging from a full commitment to autonomy to an equally passionate protection of diversity.[5] Within this range, scholars and policy makers struggle with defining the desirable expression of choice and autonomy and its complicated relations to protecting attachment and belonging.

Accepting the realities of group identification seems to be a necessary step in the discussion of individual rights and civic equality in liberal democracies. But the challenge of nonreflective communities presents itself here in full force: if some individuals are deemed to have their identity derived from traditional, existing group structures while others are assumed to be the authors of their own lives, it is hard to envision shared principles of justice and of social cooperation that would correspond with the needs and aspirations of all.

Liberal democrats thus struggle to respond to the presence of nonreflective communities in their midst. Abolishing these subgroups would be undemocratic and obviously not a real option. However, fully accommodating them seems to conflict with liberalism's requirement for autonomy. Autonomy, understood as encompassing a spectrum ranging from self-authorship to a minimal potential to appraise one's options and commitments, is viewed by many as a cornerstone of liberal democracy, underpinning its basic tenets including liberty and the legitimacy of the state.[6] When accommodated subgroups reject the notion of individual autonomy and replace it with a demand to obey traditions, elders, or customs, liberalism and liberal democracy seem to be facing some grave risks. A liberal democracy may find that authoritarian forces influence decisions made by its citizens, affecting their life plans, their preferences, and their voting patterns. Such democracy may be charged with neglecting to protect the right to liberty of those members within these groups who are not given an opportunity to express themselves or to live their lives as they see fit.

I suggest that nonreflective communities do not pose such grave risks to liberal democracy as is sometimes claimed. While idealizing the harmony and sense of belonging bestowed on members of nonreflective communities would be a mistake, similarly, so would venerating a life based on choice as the only or most fulfilling way of life, or as the only one that fully corresponds with liberal-democratic demands. Even more to the point, as argued in previous chapters, juxtaposing the two, or regarding them as mutually exclusive, would also be a mistake. The life of choice and communal life are not, in reality, two separate ways of life led by distinctly different groups. The multicultural nature of individuals' personal identity makes the moral realities of affiliation significantly messier than the distinction between the autonomous life and the nonreflective life—or general society and the nonreflective communities it encompasses—seems to suggest. This sets the stage for defending nonreflective communities as belonging with, and deserving similar treatment to, other groups in a liberal democracy.

The case in defense of nonreflective communities has been made by numerous authors, who have broadly argued that the threat posed by these communities to their members and to the general society is not as grave as some presume.[7] Devoutly religious communities, and other nonreflective groups, can still participate in many of the public practices expected of citizens. They can be aware of, and let their children become aware of, other ways of life. They often endorse their conception of the good based on a fair assessment of other options at a similar level to other citizens (that is to say, not as well as the theoretical ideal, but well enough). And they can support certain policies over others based on the congruence of these policies with their value set, like other citizens do. Finally, as both theory and available data confirm, they often can leave their communities when they so decide.

In what follows, this suggestion—that liberal democrats are sometimes too quick to demonize or dismiss nonreflective communities—is considered in light of the contemporary debate on cultural accommodation. Much of this debate focuses on women's rights as individuals, as citizens, and as members of cultural communities that may be oppressive toward women. In other cases, the debate turns to the education of children and the obligation the state has to facilitate the development of their autonomy. Both gender equality and education for autonomy (including autonomy-facilitating education) seem to align with the liberal claim for freedom and choice for all members of society. At the same time, they also threaten some cultural traditions and the prospect of cultural autonomy by intervening in traditional relations among members of cultural groups. Typically, the way out of this theoretical impasse is provided through the notion of exit rights. In the next section, I discuss the inadequacy of exit rights to provide a satisfactory solution to the matter of accommodating nonreflective cultures in liberal democracies.

Exit Rights

Many liberal scholars accept that cultural affiliations play a significant role in shaping personal makeup and largely influence individuals' choices. As K. Anthony Appiah puts it, "[W]e make choices, but we do not determine the options among which we choose."[8] Theorists of culture and cultural identity vary widely in their understanding of the ways in which culture generates the horizons of choice, and in their subsequent normative assessment of how democracies should respond to cultures and regulate them. Most agree, however, on the need for a right to exit. Even when defined or regulated in different ways, there is wide scholarly agreement that members of democratic societies must be able to exercise their right to exit cultural groups to which they belong.[9]

The concept of exit rights starts with the notion of the individual as a member of an existing, more or less well-defined group and maintains a concept of the individual as an author of her own fate. It focuses on the practical possibility of a rift between one's own preferences, beliefs, or rights, and the preferences, beliefs, or rights of one's group. Assuming the primacy of the individual over her group leads to prescribing exit rights as a just solution for such a rift. This solution allows liberal democrats to address the smaller-scale problem of persons who are dissatisfied (or worse) within their societal cultures, concurrently with a response to the problem of accommodating groups, including illiberal ones, into liberal-democratic theory and society.

But exit rights as discussed in contemporary theories tend to suffer from one of two shortcomings. First, they may amount to no more than lip service. Merely saying that individuals are to be allowed to leave their groups often does not provide those wishing to leave with a real opportunity to extract themselves from the culture in which they have spent their lives. Lacking money and other resources, unfamiliar with alternative ways of life, risking ostracism and severed ties, they can find themselves trapped in their cultures of origin without a real way out. Recognizing this difficulty, some have moved to demand that encompassing groups (including illiberal ones) provide members who wish to exit with the full opportunity to do so with little damage. While, as Jacob Levy states, a culture from which an exit has no cost cannot be considered a culture,[10] there have been significant theoretical as well as legal attempts to ensure that encompassing groups make exit a realistic, less costly option to their members.

This solution raises the second risk I point to in the debate on exit rights. While more realistic exit rights support individuals in their quest for departure, they stand the risk of intervening in encompassing and nonreflective communities to the point where such communities have little cultural autonomy left, and little ability to maintain their values and traditional ways of life. This problem is exacerbated when exit rights are understood to entail educating members of subgroups in the skills and capacities necessary for autonomy and choice. Using exit rights as a way to protect women from oppression in traditional groups entails educating women about options that could corrupt their membership in the group. Failing to thus educate them can result in their exit rights remaining a dead letter, without true impact on the lives of women in illiberal groups.[11]

Thus, when exit rights are conflated with intervention, their potential as a main tool for accommodating culture becomes questionable. Moreover, the liberal expectation that illiberal cultures institute exit rights suggests that the liberal value system is morally (or at least politically) superior to others, particularly to more traditional, religious, or encompassing ones. The institution of exit rights can be interpreted as representing a vision of the "general"— liberal, individualistic, autonomy-based—society, as a more advanced or otherwise better way of life. Because autonomy is assumed to be a key component of the democratic process, conferring legitimacy on the state and providing individuals with an opportunity to live a life of their own choice, there is indeed an inherent preference for this conception of the good over others in a liberal democracy. As many have expressed, this conception of the good need not amount to a view of the individual as atomistic, unencumbered, or detached. But it does require a vision of the individual as possessing certain skills and attitudes, related to rationality and critical capacities, that enable her to reflect on her life and choose her path.

While this argument may be politically sound, it does not necessitate significant interventions in subcultures, nor does it require all children to become autonomous. In fact, if autonomy is understood as the capacity to choose, providing the individual with an opportunity to change her cultural affiliation, and if this in turn represents a core value of "general" society, the burden must be put on general society to support its realization. This claim can be satisfied through augmenting minimal exit rights with the practices that I describe later as entrance paths, which address adults rather than children, and which are less interventionist in both family and culture than what substantial exit rights require. These practices align with structured paternalism in that they present a set of social policies that aim to expand the opportunities individuals have to experience both well-being and civic equality while leading a life they endorse.

As is probably clear by now, when exit rights are introduced into the discussion of individual and group identity in a liberal democracy, even in theories that are more sympathetic to group rights and that acknowledge the centrality of group affiliation in social and personal life, the balance is tipped—too far, I suggest—toward a strict liberal conception of the individual and society. The view of the individual as a rights bearer who is free to choose, and who existed before and exists beyond her group-related identity, gives rise to a host of problematic justice claims and social practices. As a result, a variety of group affiliations, including cultural and religious groups, are significantly compromised.

Before turning to discuss entrance paths, I briefly examine the question of the motivation to exit, or the social and psychological context in which the need to exit arises. Through this discussion, I hope to substantiate a realistic view of the individual as culturally embedded, yet maintaining the capacity to consider alternative ways of life.

Why Exit?

Leaving a culture, particularly an encompassing culture (including certain organized religions), is not a step individuals tend to take lightly. Appiah's question is appropriate here: "Is an identity group something you can simply resign from?"[12] What might be the reasons for individuals to aspire to exit a comprehensive group, one that establishes and reflects significant parts of their identity and which provides meaning and structure to many aspects of their lives? While individual motivations are probably as varied in this case as they are in any other human endeavor, the motivations for exit that are most relevant to the current discussion may be divided into two categories.

First, individuals may wish to leave a comprehensive group because some of its elements or regulating norms are discriminatory or oppressive toward them. This motivation has often been discussed in the literature, particularly in relation to women and minorities-within-minorities.[13] Second, there are those who wish to leave because they have lost some key element needed to motivate them in maintaining their affiliation. They may have lost their belief in the main tenets of the religion or value system; their sense of affiliation has been compromised for various reasons, or their support of shared goals has diminished.

How, then, is a descriptively multicultural, democratic society to address the fact that it consists of a multiplicity of cultures, and that some individuals within these cultures are oppressed by their groups' practices and traditions? How should it address individuals who are not oppressed, but simply fail to identify with the group's tenets or would, for other reasons, like to leave their group or join another group? And should the response differ according to the different motivations? The two cases are different because the first case is a case of rights being violated, demanding protection from the state to maintain civic equality, while the second is a case of choice, which does not demand such direct protection. The first requires a response based on an assumption of equal human rights for all members of society, regardless of their group affiliation. This response is what I characterize here as narrowly construed exit rights. The second requires an assumption of descriptive minimal autonomy available to most individuals within society, and subsequently puts the burden on the state to provide those individuals who wish to exit but are not oppressed with readily available forms

of entry into society, with or without stepping outside the boundaries of their original identity group. This second case falls under
the broader context of structured paternalism and the demand that
the state generate a defensible context of choice for all individuals.
Both cases assume an individuality that precedes group identity
and transcends it, while maintaining a respectful view of group affiliation (including comprehensive, illiberal, and nonreflective
groups). The challenges they present to society are different, and
the responses to those challenges should be as well.

Consider Ruth, a member of a cultural or religious group who
loses faith in some of the main tenets of her group's culture or religion and, devoid of faith, would like to abandon her community
and live a life that allows her to express her authentic, nonbelieving
self freely. She may or may not endorse alternative sets of beliefs.
Ruth wants to leave her group because she no longer identifies with
the group's tradition or mission. She finds the practices unsatisfy-
ing, maybe alienating. She no longer believes in the group's key
teachings, no longer supports its belief system, and fails to see
beauty or value in the limitations and expectations of its customs.
She cannot, as it were, endorse this way of life "from the inside."[14]

In order to exit, Ruth would probably need to leave behind
much of what is dear to her. Even if her group does not mandate, as
some groups do, that those who leave not take any property with
them, and even if her family does not renounce her, the loss will be
significant. She will no longer have the familiar, the known, the
expected, to rely on. She will no longer have some of the social ties
she had before, whether because other members reject her or because she no longer finds relations with them meaningful. Ruth
will probably need to rethink many aspects of her life and her identity—her expectations from herself and others, her future plans,
her views about a host of personal and public issues. For some ex-
members of encompassing groups, exit turns into a lifelong process of search and self-discovery.

While Ruth's path carries some strong resemblance to Millian
self-authorship, it is unclear why the state should sponsor this pro-

cess through intervening in her group's practices or ensuring a low price for her exit. Life choices of this sort, while significant for individuals, belong in the realm of personal decisions. Other decisions of this sort, such as the choice of a partner or a decision to move to another home or to divorce, are also important personal matters. They are protected by certain liberties such as the freedom of movement, and they are regulated to some extent through processes such as border control and marriage licensing. But the controls, and the liberties, come after the decision has been taken. No state intervention is expected for individuals who fail to develop, or choose not to enter, intimate relations. No supports are offered to individuals who spend their whole lives in the place where they were born and raised, whether because they choose not to move or because they are limited by their personal circumstances. There is no state support for individuals who choose to divorce, although the price of exit from marriage is often very high, as these intimate relations have often provided meaning and context, as well as emotional and financial support to all participants.[15] Similarly, state regulation and support for individuals who wish to sever their ties with their group need not take the form of encouragement to exit or provision of tools and skills to exit, as long as rights are not being violated.

But what happens when rights are in fact violated? Consider Sarah, who wishes to leave her group because it regards her as a second-rate member. In her traditional, nonreflective group, women are kept at home. They are not allowed to participate in communal decision making. Sarah is threatened by, or may be subject to physical abuse by, members of her family—a risk that increases significantly if she rebels.

If the reason for the wish to exit is oppression, clearly the liberal-democratic state is required to support the exit attempt in order to prevent or end rights infringement. As in the cases offered in previous chapters for protecting children and vulnerable family members, the protection of rights is the first line of response in the state's obligation toward all its members. In a debate on exit rights that is limited to these cases, there is little need to extend basic rights beyond existing legal and other mechanisms to protect the rights of all individuals in democracy. Narrow exit rights, based on the rights that all members of society have, including those who are oppressed by their communities, do not require changes in existing legal and conceptual frameworks. Narrow exit rights are limited to the protection of basic human rights through legal and other forms of protection to individuals whose rights are being violated within their groups.

Many scholarly debates go much further. They suggest that in order to escape rights violations and oppression, the state must require that Sarah and Ruth be educated so they can be informed about their rights and equal worth as human beings, and to do that they must learn about other options, other cultures, and other ways of life. They must be allowed by the group to own property so that they are not impoverished if they decide to leave. And the group may be required to put aside some funds to support those who decide to opt out.

Note, though, that supporting Sarah through instituting narrow exit rights is a clear requirement from a state that endorses human rights as part of its basic structure, through constitutional assurances or other tools. This requirement should not be conflated with supporting Ruth, which represents taking a few steps further in the direction of instituting liberal-democratic values for all. This type of state intervention in subgroup cultures—the mandated removal of economic barriers to exit, the requirement of autonomy-facilitating education, and other substantive aspects of exit rights—requires an argument that presents autonomy and choice not only as core values of democracy, but also as ones that trump many others. To require institutional structures that support Ruth, the argument for autonomy must be one that regards Ruth's opportunity to choose her cultural context as more important than her peers' and family's (and possibly her own) preference for harmony and belonging. Such arguments are problematic in terms of the level of intervention in subgroups that they require, and the narrow, imposing vision of liberal democracy they rely on.

Clearly, the two motivations can be mixed, such as when one loses her faith because of her sense that the group is unjust in its treatment of certain members (possibly including herself), or when one is oppressed because she does not present the expected levels of commitment to the group's main tenets. Liberal democrats who are concerned with adaptive preferences may be wary of the distinction between Sarah and Ruth. They may suggest that the state should take a more active role in protecting all who wish to leave, because the decision to stay could be inauthentic, a function of accommodating oneself to a bad situation. But this concern, while valid, does not undermine the distinction between rights violation and preferences, which the two cases of Ruth and Sarah are meant to represent. If the adaptive preferences are a result of years of oppression, which left their mark on one's ability to fathom a better life, the state's obligation is to intervene and support the oppressed member(s), as part of the general commitment of a democratic state to protect its members' rights. If the decision to stay, or to leave, is a result of other forces shaping one's preferences, the state should respect that decision as it should respect other choices that individuals make for a variety of reasons, both reasonable and unreasonable, known and unknown to the individual, wholehearted and half-hearted, autonomous and heteronomous. The state should respond by providing structured paternalist processes, and in this case specifically by providing, beyond rights protection, entrance paths. Those are institutions and regulations that can contribute to the host of forces shaping one's view of what is possible and what could be preferred.

Where does this critical discussion of exit rights lead? If exit rights alone do not solve the problem they set out to address, namely, the need to protect individuals while accommodating group identity in a liberal-democratic society, and if in their robust form they maintain a comprehensive liberal view that offers little cultural accommodation, the need for an alternative becomes clear. In the following section, I suggest that a narrow form of exit rights, one that protects against gross human rights violations, should be augmented with additional institutional support for exiting members of illiberal groups, namely, entrance paths. Entrance paths are suggested here as an appropriate response to many of Ruth's needs as well as to some of Sarah's without the problematic consequences of intervention that substantial exit rights necessitate.

Entrance Paths

The question that stands at the origins of the debate on exit rights and cultural accommodation is, again, how is the liberal-democratic state to respond to the presence of encompassing cultural groups within liberal society in a way that respects their way of life yet protects the rights of individuals within them?

The answer to this question should focus not merely on exit but also on entrance. In other words, it should not focus on intervening in subcultures for the purpose of changing or regulating them, but rather on creating new structures within liberal democracy that can provide support mechanisms for individuals who prefer ways of life other than the ones in which they were raised. While some theorists (Chandran Kukathas is a notable example) grant that the right to exit must have a related point of entry to complement it, the implications of this complementary view have not significantly affected the discussion of exit rights. Admittedly, entrance is in many ways simply the other side of exit, and is assumed in more substantial discussions of exit rights (as distinct from thin or formal ones). However, focusing on entrance has moral as well as practical advantages. By accepting that the idea of culture presupposes some cost to exit, liberal theorists focus on reducing the cost to individuals who exit from illiberal, nonreflective, and oppressive groups. However, little attention has been given to reducing the cost of entrance into an alternative group, or into mainstream society if it is not characterized as a group in itself. Learning new ways of being, acquiring new skills, social ties, and capital, sometimes a new language—all these have material and other costs that must be considered in creating a full account of exit. These costs burden Ruth as well as Sarah—the nature of the motivation for exit is inconsequential to the price of entrance.

Exit rights may provide an opportunity to abandon oppressive or otherwise unfulfilling conditions and exchange them for an abstract form of freedom, but they offer little direction as to the navigation of this freedom. Liberal theorists tend to assume that freedom is its own reward, that leaving behind an oppressive life or a life built on a value set not endorsed by the individual provides in itself an opportunity to thrive. This view is well supported by the classical liberal focus on the individual and on the ideal of self-authorship. It meshes well with a vision of society as composed entirely of individuals who exchange positions, views, and property with each other.

But once groups, belonging, and affiliation are introduced, this view of society becomes imbalanced. To correct this imbalance, we need to start with a practical vision of what it means to leave a cultural group. The possibility of leaving presupposes the existence of some other groups in the same society that are open to new members, or a general society that is only loosely formed and which is centered more significantly on an individualistic conception of its members. The members of this society of individuals still have traditions and affiliations, but they are assumed to be less encompassing than those of comprehensive cultures.[16]

In addition, it is worth noting that in many cases, moving from one group to the next does not make one a regular member of the group one has entered, even when the new group is as seemingly loosely organized as mainstream liberal-democratic society. A person's upbringing and her original affiliations stay with her in many ways. Some of these ways are harder to shed, such as when group affiliation is based on race, language, or ethnicity. Further features are more than skin deep and remain central to many individuals' identity as they make a new life outside their original group. Many will always remain related to their culture of origin, with the prefix "former" attached to their self-identifying title, as well as to their identification by others. For all these reasons, the institution of entrance paths, as relevant forms of structured paternalist social policies, is critical to the practical possibility of exchanging one's cultural affiliation. This is true for individuals who wish to move away from their current group for reasons unrelated to oppression and is potentially helpful also for those who wish to escape oppressive cultures (but augments rather than substitutes rights protection). But even in cases of rights protection, entrance paths are needed to supplement other, more intrusive forms of intervention and protection.

This change of perspective—from subgroups and exit to broader society and entrance—is justified for a number of reasons. First, if autonomy and choice are valued by mainstream liberal society but not, or less so, by nonreflective subgroups, then the burden of realizing these values should fall on general society rather than on the subgroups. That is because realizing these values provides mainstream society with greater ethical and other benefits. Ayelet Shachar argues that in the context of oppressed individuals, the burden of exit should not fall on individuals' shoulders:

> The "right of exit" solution similarly fails to provide a comprehensive answer. Instead, it throws upon the already beleaguered individual the responsibility to either miraculously transform the legal-institutional conditions that keep her vulnerable or to find the resources to leave her whole world behind. Surely it is troubling when a solution demands that those who are the most vulnerable must pay the highest price, while the abusers remain undisturbed.[17]

The same argument should hold for burdens placed on cultural groups that may be marginalized or discriminated against, or that for various reasons reject the values of choice and autonomy (or do not give them a central role in their belief systems). Exit rights in their substantial form demand that they change their practices in ways that may contribute to their weakening (because of waning membership) or demise (by undermining their belief systems). Alternatively, a focus on entrance paths into the general society puts less of a burden on subgroups and more on the institutions representing the majority and expressing the main liberal-democratic belief system.

Second, focusing on general society and on entrance is justified because it expresses an acknowledgment of the importance of cultural belonging for individual well-being, while still retaining a view of the individual as transcending her cultural group. This respect for individuals as both "embedded" and "authors of their own lives" is possible in this view because it maximizes the noninterventionist stance of the liberal-democratic state, allowing cultural groups to maintain their traditional ways of life, while at the same time respecting and supporting individuals who choose to leave and responding to their needs and well-being (as paternalist policies regularly do). And while this approach supports individuals in leaving their comprehensive group, it does not assume that they do so for the purpose of becoming entirely unaffiliated; rather, it recognizes the importance of supporting the development of new contexts of belonging.

Moreover, the focus on entrance rather than on exit alone allows the discussion to concentrate on adults rather than children as the relevant constituency for these policies. The discussion of cultural accommodation and choice has long been mired in the debate over parental rights and family prerogatives. It is hard to foresee an argument for intervention in children's opportunities to explore alternative cultural options that will not encounter a vehement response by proponents of family cohesion and parental rights; many of these arguments are not only convincing in their own right but also hard to counter both morally and politically. A focus on entrance paths, and subsequently on adults who wish to exit rather than on teaching children that they should consider exit, provides a way out of this impasse.

What do entrance paths require? How should they be organized, and what institutional forms might they take? In some cases, entrance paths into mainstream society already exist, although they are not framed in this way. The clearest case of these paths is judicial recourse, the opportunity to turn to the courts when one believes that her rights have been violated. This tool is sometimes used in an attempt to minimize interventions in traditional groups (as in both the *Yoder* and the *Mozert* cases).[18] But at other times, it is used to bring about change in one's group of origin, and to allow individuals who are oppressed within their group and wish to either change it or leave it a way to do so at a lesser cost (as in the case of Julia Martinez).[19] The fact that all members of a liberal democracy can bring their claims before a court provides not only a rights protection tool but also an important potential formal entrance path to members of subgroups, particularly those who are oppressed.

Other institutions can participate in providing entrance paths into society for those who are considering moving away from their group of origin, or are looking for new attachments and affiliations. The state can support organizations of former members of subgroups, which are often the best entrance ports into general society, especially for those coming from encompassing groups. Ex-Mormons, like ex-Amish and ex-members of the Jewish Ultra-Orthodox community, for example, often maintain an identity of former members after they leave. They organize to ease exit and entrance, and provide much-needed means of support—material, informational, and emotional—to fellow ex-members. The state can support these groups through providing materials resources—for example, through tax exemptions. It can also support their linkage with existing health and welfare institutions, as much as they are interested in such ties, to provide access to further modes of support. This is a metaphoric underground railroad, which, through the structured paternalist support of the state, can become an effective way of augmenting exit rights with entrance paths.

Welfare institutions should take into account the special needs of these individuals, who can be seen as new immigrants into society, even if they did not cross international borders to get into their new homes. Thinking back to the *Yoder* case, the institution of entrance paths would mean that the state of Wisconsin could have responded to the Amish exemption from the last two years of compulsory education by establishing a fund to support state-sponsored adult education for those who leave school before attaining a high school diploma, including ex-Amish, who later in life are struggling to enter the workforce (and possibly to join the engaged public). Other existing structures—some public, some private—that are aimed at supporting immigrants can be used, or replicated, to support this form of internal migration across groups and value systems. Examples are specialized responses to the health needs of those who are exiting traditional societies, support in navigating the housing market and financial institutions, and other related forms of assistance that can sometimes be found in "immigrant clinics." Jeff Spinner-Halev acknowledges the need for such support and its practical implications: "To enable people to leave by easing the transition to the outside world, the Hutterites [but not the Amish or Ultra-Orthodox because they can own property and save money] should set aside a small fund for members who leave their community.... No one should become wealthy by leaving, but a few thousand dollars would help members leave the community if they wish."[20] While I agree with Spinner-Halev that support for the transition out is necessary, it is not the Hutterites that should provide this assistance. Mainstream society and its formal institutions should provide these supports rather than burdening subgroups through intervention and regulation. Therefore, support should apply to individuals coming from groups that allow them to own property as much as it should apply to others who become impoverished by their exit. They would need different forms of support, but its location and structure remain constant across these different cases. This is a special case to which the general justifications for structured paternalism apply, and that requires implementation through specific procedures and institutions.

To illustrate using Spinner-Halev's example, the fund to support exiting Hutterites should be a public fund rather than a government-required Hutterite fund. The Hutterites are paying the price of exit by losing members, giving up attachments, and weakening their already marginal value system and group. General society is gaining new members as well as further support for its already triumphant values. Thus, it can afford, and should be expected to pay (materially and otherwise), for this benefit.

But should the state be also required, or allowed, to teach the Hutterite children, and children from other encompassing groups, that they can exit? Should it encourage them to consider this option? In the next section, I focus on a key issue in this debate—education—and examine its role in accommodating cultures through exit rights or through entrance paths.

Entrance Paths: The Case of Schooling

Public schools seem to offer a solution to the question of cultural accommodation. For many liberal democrats, schooling is a natural arena in which to address some of the elements of accommodation and integration because, since children are already compelled to attend school, promoting liberal values there would not involve any additional intrusion into the private sphere. While the social effects of this exposure may still be controversial, particularly because of its "spillover effect,"[21] the actual practice is less worrisome to most scholars because it addresses children.

The contours of the liberal-democratic argument on education as it relates to exit rights are roughly as follows: for exit rights to do what they are meant to do for liberal-democratic theory and policy, they must be available not only in principle but also in practical terms. In other words, they must be made available to all members of all cultural groups within society, who must be aware of them, be able to appreciate them, and be able to exercise them. For this to happen, a number of interventions by the state into societal (and other) cultural groups would be required, first and foremost in the form of education for all members. This education must lead all members to know about and appreciate their opportunity to exit. They must hence know of other possible ways of life and how to access them. And they must possess the skills and knowledge necessary for exiting, should they choose to.

But should schools in fact be participating in the process of cultural integration? Is it justified that public schools, as public social-political institutions, take part in teaching children about their opportunities to secede from their cultures?

Some theorists answer in the affirmative, claiming that in fact this is one of the main charges of schools as public institutions. Exposing children to other cultures is suggested as a way to generate tolerance, a key aspect of democratic society, but also to facilitate autonomy and develop critical capacities in children.[22] These are sometimes used as key justifications for publicly funding schools. In Michael Hand's terms, schools are charged with developing dispositional autonomy in children (or the inclination to determine one's own actions), and this mandate is crucial in the area of advancing their circumstantial autonomy (or the condition of being free to determine one's own actions).[23] In other words, if children learn to be autonomous, they may well reject cultural and religious contexts in which they are not free to exercise this autonomy, thus endorsing free society over their more limiting cultural contexts.

These schooling practices are thought to protect individual rights and civic equality, while at the same time replicating the main tenets of a liberal society by teaching children to endorse liberal views such as gender and racial equality. Schooling carries the potential to liberate individuals from oppressive cultures where their rights are trampled—for example, to liberate women and girls from cultural groups that regard them as inferior and that minimize their opportunities; at the same time, it is meant to support the prospects of affecting change in these cultures by introducing their members to other, presumably more desirable ways of thinking that are based on civic equality and nondiscrimination.

In addition to these important values, many authors give diversity a main role in the formation of good citizenship through schooling. Putting children from many backgrounds under the same educational roof is important not only for the sake of equality. Teaching them all about their respective cultures is not justified only on the basis of recognition and self-respect, although all of these justifications are important and are often part of the argument. But the common argument contains another key element: it suggests that the encounter among different cultures, ways of life, and conceptions of the good, and a curriculum that reflects the histories and values of these different ways of life, can support a substantive opportunity for children to choose ways of life other than their families'. It is suggested that this vision of school as a "great sphere," in Bruce Ackerman's terms, provides children with a desirable opportunity to consider the set of values parents and communities aim to instill in them, thereby giving them a chance to decide for themselves about their own conception of the good.

This line of argument, I suggest, goes too far in the direction of intervention and should not be endorsed by liberal democrats who are committed to cultural diversity and tolerance. Public education should not be considered a key part of the response to the challenge of cultural accommodation. The protection of human rights is a sound reason for imposing intrusive policies on cultural minorities, but the education of children should not be considered part of this endeavor. Because education for cultural freedom (or autonomy) is aimed at individuals like Ruth (who lost their faith) and not at those in Sarah's condition (whose rights are being violated), its provision should not be a prerogative, or a responsibility, of the state. Moreover, if the state does step in and provides "great sphere" education, or education for autonomy and cultural choice, it stands at risk of trespassing cultural boundaries in ways that undermine its mission of respect for diverse visions of the good life, without appropriate justification.

Take as another example the traditional education of some Jewish Ultra-Orthodox girls, which requires them to be shielded from the corrupting influences of non-Orthodox society. In its extreme form, it requires that they learn only what is necessary for fulfilling their future roles as homemakers. Substantial exit rights of the kind criticized here would necessitate intervention in their education. These girls would have to be exposed to other ways of life, and learn to question their own, thus corrupting their belief system and perceived purity. They would need to learn "general education" curricula, such as math and English (particularly in communities that function in languages that are not useful for individuals who choose to exit, such as Yiddish). This education will provide them with the tools to exit if they so wish when they grow up. But it will also put them in a different position at present, and could undermine the cultural and religious project their families are engaged in. It is unlikely that parents and community leaders would endorse this kind of education for girls. If some girls or their families would choose such an education, this might in itself indicate a form of exit, creating a difference and a distance from the rest of the community. The girls may be deemed undesirable for marriage, which is a damning label in a closed, traditional community. The leaders and some parents may reasonably oppose this kind of education, as Shelly Burtt has asserted, because "[w]hat we see as intolerance of differing views of the world is, from this perspective, fear of the corruption of faith."[24]

Thus, contrary to widespread assumptions, education for autonomy (including autonomy-facilitating education) may carry devastating consequences for individuals and groups and may undermine the project of cultural accommodation. Beyond these undesirable consequences for individuals and for the moral standing of the state, this form of education is not demanded by liberal-democratic values, if the distinction between the two different motivations to leave—Ruth's and Sarah's—is kept in mind. The Ultra-

Orthodox girls may not be given a full set of opportunities to develop certain dimensions of their values and perceptions. They may be facing a narrow field of professional opportunities, and they may have other significant restrictions on their freedom of choice. But their condition, I argue, does not amount to a violation of human rights. It is rather a form of value set that should be endorsed by those who favor value pluralism, and thus does not require the state to step in and protect them. Their situation can be partially compared to the condition of spiritually inclined children of liberal parents, who are not comprehensively exposed to the potential benefits of religious ways of life. While their current worldview and options are diminished in this way, they are still able to move between value systems as they grow. The limiting of current exposure thus does not warrant the imposition of autonomy-facilitating education. Therefore, mandating autonomy-facilitating education is unjustified by arguments pertaining to exit. Moreover, even if mandated, it would only reach some, and arguably it will fail to reach those who are assumed to need it most, as they—members of oppressive communities—may well be attending private schools (including homeschools) that cater to their worldview. Thus, under current social conditions, education for autonomy and "great sphere" education in the public schools cannot satisfy the demands of accommodation, or those of liberalism.

These concerns are at stake even when more extreme groups are discussed, and the concerns are clearly pressing in the context of parents and communities aiming to preserve a religious way of life. These communal views are reasonable enough to be accommodated within a liberal framework. Burtt rightly observes that when properly understood as concerns about grace rather than as uncivic perspectives on autonomy, "the concerns of especially devout parents no longer present as great a challenge to liberal-democratic norms as some suppose."[25] If that is indeed an accurate depiction of the concerns raised by devout, religious, or nonreflective parents, then the focus on children and schools as the locus of exit rights is misguided. The focus should rather be on those individuals who have abandoned their beliefs and are considering or seeking other value systems.

The argument for autonomy-developing and autonomy-facilitating education as a way to introduce cultural "options" seems to be distorted in that, in Charles Taylor's words, it misinterprets choice as a good in itself. Its focus on autonomy as self-authorship fails to acknowledge the importance of distinguishing between those who would leave their groups to escape oppression and those who may develop a preference for another culture as part of an existential process.

Politically speaking, the emphasis on the opportunity to switch cultures stands at risk of alienating from mainstream society any and all members of those cultures who believe that their set of values is indeed reflective of the truth. Devout religious sects would likely be suspicious of institutions that aim to support their children in a journey outside their belief system. Other groups that are committed to a definitive set of values may share this concern.

But the critique of the great sphere argument goes beyond the political calculation of those who might support or reject it. The concerns of religious communities and families, such as those in the *Yoder* and *Mozert* cases, should be considered—and are in fact very widely discussed in the liberally oriented scholarly debate—because of the importance of the perspective they raise. While schools are indeed charged with widening students' horizons, and while they should indeed support the development of critical capacities, directing much of these efforts toward one's culture or religion seems to miss the point. A devotion to one set of values may be disconcerting to those who believe in the democratic power of choice, but choice should not be construed as the opportunity to abandon your way of life for another. The rejection of the set of values one was raised with is a possibility that should not be denied, but neither should it be an aim of democratic schooling. The focus of public schooling should not be the endorsement of choice through a vision of a great sphere or other institutional arrangements aimed at providing a critical distance between individuals and their upbringing. Again, I agree with Burtt's statement that "[i]f children are truly to have the choice of a strong religious faith, their early contact with the pluralistic and secular values of a modern society must be guarded and carefully supervised."[26]

If they do not wish to argue for abolishing religion and nonreflective cultures, liberal democrats must acknowledge that public schools—like society itself—can accommodate a variety of affiliations without serious concerns to the well-being of democracy or its members. Their aspiration should not be to introduce, or instill, the possibility of self-authorship or even a more minimal version of autonomy.[27] The reflection on the practices each child is raised to endorse should not be considered part of the role of a democratic public education system. As long as children are able to participate as civic equals—a requirement that should be understood procedurally rather than as a matter of soul-crafting—their particular affiliations are beyond the realm of justified public (including educational) intervention.

The argument against providing the conditions for exit rights through schooling thus becomes, in essence, an argument against autonomy-facilitating education. In one of the strongest and most widely cited arguments for such education, Harry Brighouse suggests that autonomy-facilitating education is to be considered part of the state's obligations toward all children.[28] Such education would allow children the basis for autonomous preference formation and affirmation, and it would support the development of skills that may enable all children to choose the life that is good for them. Asserting that the process of how to live well is at least partially known and is related to the ability to rationally assess options, and that the needs of children in the modern world are at least partially well defined (navigating changing social conditions, accommodating new technologies), Brighouse concludes that all children should be exposed to autonomy-facilitating education, because many of them will require it in order to live a good life. Therefore, providing all children with the skills to develop this autonomous way of conducting their lives is required of the state as part of its fulfillment of the condition of justice. This argument requires the endorsement of a thick vision of liberalism and of autonomy, and in a way necessitates the rejection of nonreflective or otherwise encompassing ways of life. Simply put, Brighouse's argument for the centrality of autonomy-facilitating education for equal civic standing is premised on the suggestion that a life of choice is better than other ways of life and, therefore, that soul-crafting that enables a life of choice is a necessary aspect of liberal-democratic governance. I argue here for a thinner version of the liberal-democratic response to cultural difference, one that I find more appealing, but also which is more likely to be part of an overlapping consensus, and which provides a more appropriate answer to the challenge of cultural accommodation. This version does not require autonomy facilitation or exposure to alternative ways of life beyond promoting the democratic aim of tolerance; it does not seek to encourage all individuals within society to become autonomous authors of their lives. Rather, it suffices with opening paths of entry to those who wish to exit their communities as independent individuals—as adults (or older adolescents).

Is that not too late in life, some may ask? In his discussion of exposure to religious alternatives in education, Emile Lester has suggested that education for autonomy be directed toward "the more modest goal of ensuring that students have a reasonable ability to exit from their communities when they feel that membership has become excessively painful."[29] This suggestion requires exposing older students, at the high school level, to alternative religious views, so as to let them know that other visions and other possibilities of salvation are available. Lester hopes that students would use this knowledge to exit their group in extreme cases when they can no longer endure membership in their religious group of origin. This moderate form of autonomy focused on the knowledge of other options and the ability to extract oneself from one's group of upbringing is indeed necessary in any account of exit. If one's mind is entirely taken over by externally enforced views offered by parents, elders, or the scriptures, and one is completely unable to see any alternative or has no knowledge that other groups exist, no route for exit (or entry) would be of any help. I suggest (along with others, notably Spinner-Halev) that this moderate form of autonomy, which is based on having a basic knowledge about other options, is available to most all members of subgroups even without state intervention and education for autonomy. I further suggest that for groups who are extreme and isolated to the extent that their members, or some of them, have no knowledge of outside groups, the state cannot affect them by the measures discussed here or in other liberal-democratic literature. The main tools available in dealing with such groups are letting them alone or breaking them up—and both options carry a high price. Lester's modest argument is helpful in pointing out that in groups that are not fully isolated and dominating, there is no need for early intervention in creating "autonomy skills"; opportunities for practicing one's preferences would do for most individuals, and they would satisfy liberal-democratic principles. Providing these opportunities would require less intervention in nonreflective communities, and more structural changes in the direction of accommodating the needs of members who are either contemplating exit or have already chosen to exit their comprehensive communities. In other words, going back to the general theme of this book, opportunities rather than autonomy should be the focus of structured paternalist policies addressing members of comprehensive groups.

This skepticism toward the need for autonomy-facilitating education may seem to echo a support for a different view on liberalism. Contrary to the autonomy-based argument, political liberalism (or diversity liberalism) prefers the protection of culture over the protection of certain rights of individuals within cultures: "[L]iberalism is about the protection of diversity, not the valorization of choice."[30] Galston offers a forceful argument for preserving diversity and thus rejecting autonomy facilitation through education, as this newly acquired autonomy might spill over to individuals' personal lives and undermine their capability to "live their lives in ways that express their deepest beliefs about what gives meaning or value to life."[31] While my argument leans more toward this form of liberalism, and favors an understanding of the democratic project as diversity-based rather than autonomy-based, it is important to note that my aim is not to develop a defense of diversity liberalism. Beyond their significant differences, both liberal views—autonomy liberalism and diversity liberalism—share a commitment to exit rights that fails to acknowledge the distinction between motivations for exit, a distinction crucial to the justified institution of both accommodating and intrusive practices. Galston maintains that "enforcement of basic rights of citizenship and of exit rights, suitably understood, will usually suffice" for the purpose of enforcing basic liberties.[32] Spinner-Halev, despite his convincing claim that "[i]nternal and external restrictions are necessary for a community to retain its identity,"[33] and his subsequent support for accommodating restrictive communities, maintains that the condition of independence must be safeguarded, "as it ensures that no one in the community is coerced. In sum, there must be a real right of exit."[34]

As indicated, I suggest that this focus on exit is misplaced. One of its most undesirable effects is a focus on educating young children for awareness of other cultural options, other conceptions of the good, and the development of related skills to pursue these options. Individuals in liberal societies, even those in closed, encompassing communities, usually know what is around them. They know that other people practice other ways of living. They are aware of the general contours of other options (even if in idealized or demonized forms). As Spinner-Halev recognizes, "Most religious conservatives, even those in insular groups, know they have a choice about their lives and so meet the minimal requirements of liberal autonomy. They see other people around them living different kinds of lives. Members of insular groups leave all the time. Members of these groups may have psychological difficulties in leaving their community . . . but there is little that liberalism can do about that."[35] Recent empirical data make evident that at least in the religious context of the United States, many people not only

118

have knowledge of other options but also take advantage of the opportunity to switch religions.[36] Close to 44 percent of adults in the United States today are not practicing the religion in which they were raised.[37] The group that gains the largest portion of these movements is the "unaffiliated" group. This description coincides with the description of mainstream society as liberal and individualistic (although in the United States, only 16 percent of adults describe themselves as unaffiliated, casting doubt over the thicker individualistic description of mainstream society). While leaving a religion and leaving a cultural community are not always equivalent processes, these numbers offer some validation to the suggestion that individuals know that they can exit, and they tend to have the minimal skills required for exit. What they often lack, I argue, is support for this process. This support can be provided in structurally paternalist ways through the institution of entrance paths.

Therefore, entrance paths should focus on those adults who already wish to exit, and offer initiating opportunities to new or aspiring members. A key way to do this would be through adult education, which would provide knowledge and skills to former members of cultures who were not exposed to the general knowledge required for participation in the general society. To go back to the example of the Ultra-Orthodox Jewish community, former members of this community may need language courses if they grew up speaking Yiddish, or they may find it useful to learn history and civics if they went to an educational institution that focused on religious rather than general subjects. New members of mainstream society may be assisted via professional development or work preparation courses. The state can help by providing support to employers who are willing to initiate these internal immigrants into the workforce. Organizations of ex-members should receive public support (possibly in the form of tax breaks for professional development or related activities) as a way to express general society's willingness to accept them into its ranks, and to share some of the burden that results from the process of exit.

All of these policies are ways of welcoming new members, of

accepting their decision to exchange one cultural affiliation with another, and of supporting them in the process of becoming members-at-large of a liberal democracy. Such policies are not meant to encourage more exit, but rather to indicate the willingness to support those who wish to exit and to share the price of their decision. Lack of entrance paths can be a strong deterrent to exiting, possibly as formidable as the original community's efforts to keep its members in. If a liberal democracy aims to express support for the idea that all individuals should be allowed to change their cultural affiliations, it should start by providing support to those who would like to join its loosely organized public space.

In sum, adult education, broadly construed, along with some other mechanisms that address adults, should be viewed as a key liberal-democratic response to encompassing cultures and preferred over the schooling of children for autonomy, because (1) pragmatically, many members of encompassing cultures use private and homeschools; (2) morally, autonomy should not be considered a value that trumps other contradictory values; and (3) it is more effective, as well as more justified politically and morally, to focus on adults who wish to leave rather than on children whose affiliations are not yet fully formed.

Conclusion: Bearing the Burden of Exit

Exit rights are a form of intervention espoused by liberal democrats as a way to sustain a commitment to individualism while accommodating group affiliation within a democracy. I have argued that the literature on this matter has been skewed to supporting intervention and state coercion more than is required or justified. To correct that tendency, narrow exit rights that aim at protecting human rights should be augmented with policies and state actions, dubbed here entrance paths, that do not carry the moral costs of intervention while providing similar (or preferable) benefits.

Exit, as an expression of personal choice, is a key aspect of the contemporary liberal-democratic approach to accommodating minority cultures, particularly nonreflective ones. It is a way for liberal democracies to express their endorsement of choice as a value and as a desirable practice for all members. Positioning exit as a key right for members of minority groups seems to allow liberal democrats to maintain their endorsement of diversity while preserving their commitment to individual choice and self-authorship, autonomy, and freedom. However, these values, and exit as a manifestation of them, are not similarly positioned as a key feature of some comprehensive and nonreflective cultures.[38] Consequently, the burden of realizing values such as freedom, self-authorship, and autonomy should first and foremost be assigned to the liberal-democratic, or general, society. Bearing the burden of fulfilling these values (or expressing them in the basic structure of society) means, first, that the liberal-democratic institutions' responsibility is to provide all members with an opportunity to realize their conception of the good. In the context of accommodating minority cultures, including illiberal comprehensive cultures, the notion of choice and exit should be expressed mainly through opening entrance paths for members of minority cultures into general society. Distinguishing between different motivations for exit, particularly between oppression-based and preference-based motivations, can direct liberal democrats in instituting relevant corresponding policies. In particular, it should direct them toward establishing narrow exit rights that protect individuals against oppression, along with more robust entrance paths that can assist exiting individuals of whatever motivation.

Liberal democracies, particularly when viewed through the lens of opportunity and diversity rather than that of choice and autonomy, do not require a full implementation of the conditions of exit rights, including autonomy-facilitating education and intervention in communal practices that may hinder choice and exit. Beyond preventing human rights violations and responding to the needs of oppressed minorities-within-minorities, the main commitment of a liberal-democratic society is to provide entrance paths to individuals who wish to pursue a different form of life outside their communities of origin. Ethical individualism, or the vision that the individual rather than the group or state is the basic unit of our analysis, is maintained as part of the foundations of this view. This priority of the individual does not eliminate the importance of cultural affiliation and other group relations in a democracy. It does not mean that the individual is the only unit of moral analysis, but that she is the agent for which social policies—including laws—are constructed. Placing individuals as the first reference point allows for a social priority set in which a society can strike a balance between individual preferences and the preservation of social affiliations that allow for the fulfillment of certain ways of life. Advocating entrance paths rather than relying solely on exit rights allows the theory and practice of the state to remain committed to the view that individuals are to be regarded as masters of their lives. It requires the state to maintain a commitment to accommodating a wide range of visions of the good life as understood by individuals and expressed in their lives, activities, and affiliations. And it requires that the state shares the responsibility for allowing individuals to pursue their vision of the good life, as an acknowledgment of the state's role in generating the conditions into which individuals are born, and the options from which they can choose. Sharing this responsibility is possible through the structured paternalist practices that provide entrance paths for those who wish to enter.

To open entrance paths while accommodating a wide range of established conceptions of the good, liberal democracies should focus on adults rather than on children. Their role should not be viewed as emphasizing the development of skills and attitudes that enable or encourage choice in the form of exit. What liberal-democratic theory and practice should focus on, rather, is easing the transition from encompassing communities to general society by providing exiting individuals clear routes for entry, support in adjustment, and opportunities to become full members in their newly chosen community.

—⚹— 6 —⚹—

SCHOOL CHOICE AS A BOUNDED IDEAL

IN PREVIOUS CHAPTERS, I have suggested that choice is sometimes presented as a panacea to social and educational problems. This is the case in the debate on school choice as well. From staunch defenders of small government and nonintervention who believe that the benefits of private markets can be extended into the public domain through choice policies, to egalitarians who worry about social justice, arguments for the advantage of individual choice over regulation and intervention abound.[1] An additional line of the moral-political debate on school choice has focused on parental authority versus the state's mandate over children's schooling,[2] with advocates of both perspectives arguing their positions with reference to the advancement of children's and parents' opportunities to develop and practice freedom and autonomy. My aim in this chapter is to examine choice policies in light of empirical evidence on choice as a personal (or freedom-enhancing) and as a social (or justice-enhancing) process. I use the discussion of school choice policies to argue that the assumption of rationality as a basis for choice in public policy making does not properly correspond with empirical studies of either rationality or choice.[3] Consequently, the theoretical models of the individual and her actions in a free, democratic context are often unfounded or misguided, as are corresponding policies. The literature on rationality and choice can shed a different light on the liberal-democratic debate on choice, autonomy, and freedom in the context of school choice. Through these connections, I offer a stronger (though admittedly messier) perspective for thinking about choice in public policy.

School choice is a prominent example of choice-based social policies. Its rationale is related to promoting two important policy goals: first, it is assumed that school choice can improve the control of individuals over the realization of their preferences, thus enhancing autonomy (or put differently, minimizing external—in this case, governmental—intervention). The general hypothesis is that "given choice parents will 'shop around,' gathering information about the quality of services schools offer, and choose carefully among their expanded set of alternatives."[4] Second, the suggestion has been made that school choice can create competition and thus improve quality, which is related to advancing egalitarian social justice goals: "Educational choice is important for two reasons. First, it extends civil rights and social justice. Second, it enhances school effectiveness. The introduction of opportunity scholarships in the District [of Columbia] comes 50 years after the *Brown v. Board of Education* decision. . . . Opportunity scholarships help remove the chains of bureaucracy. They free low-income students to obtain a better education in a school of their choosing."[5]

The combination of these elements is assumed to be supportive of social equality, in that it provides equal choice (or equal freedom) to all. These are main assumptions of the liberal (both egalitarian and libertarian) debate on school choice. In what follows, I focus on school choice as a widely debated and sporadically implemented choice policy, and consider studies that analyze the ability of parents to effectively gather information and choose well among their children's schooling options. I rely on bounded rationality literature to suggest that the ability of individuals to choose under existing conditions of school choice policies is significantly restricted. I exemplify this reality with the aid of ethnographic studies on families in the process of choosing schools for their children. The investigation of choice processes in families that are given an opportunity to choose further informs the discussion of choice as a normative political concept. This chapter suggests that bringing empirical evidence to bear on these aims informs an alternative approach to school choice and to choice policies in general. A realistic look at the cognitive and social processes of choice making points to the need to put more emphasis on structured paternalist policies including information provision, carefully designed choice sets, and other factors that respond to the realities of choosing a school.

Choice as Act and Norm in Liberal Theory

As has been discussed in previous chapters, liberal theories are interested in choice as a tool to enhance both personal freedom and social justice. A significant flaw of the liberal debate on choice in its various versions is its reliance on thin, and mostly inadequate, descriptions of social and psychological processes of choice. The main shortcoming of this underlying description is the assumption that individuals can, and in fact do, make choices in ways that are compatible with some version of Kant-inspired rationality and Mill-inspired autonomy. The rationality assumed by most liberal authors is loosely based on Kant's understanding of practical reason as the process by which we espouse maxims and judge our options in terms of their adherence to the maxims we hold. "[T]he power to judge autonomously—that is, freely (according to principles of thought in general)—is called reason."[6]

I would like to question the empirical adequacy of the common uses of this conception of the chooser, and consequently the moral as well as pragmatic standing of policies that rely on the skewed interpretation of the choosing person. While related criticisms have been raised by economic studies and recognized by some sociologists of education, still "advocates of choice and choice theories tend to rely on narrow rational and utilitarian conceptualizations of the chooser."[7] A more coherent and well-grounded view of the cognitive processes involved in choosing can better inform choice policies. In addition, a close consideration of the complicated mechanisms that take place within families as they choose schools for their children can clarify how the freedom- and autonomy-facilitating aspects of choice policies are lost in implementation.

How Individuals Make Choices

As briefly described in previous chapters, advocates of choice sometimes suggest that choosing increases the level of control that individuals—agents, consumers, and citizens in general—have over outcomes. As Keith Dowding puts it, "[O]ne of the reasons for valuing increased choice in areas of state provision is that it is supposed to increase the control of the citizens of that provision."[8] This is the policy-related expression of what liberal theory tends to describe as the opportunity to express one's preferences in the public domain. The act(s) of fulfilling one's aims are assumed to be reflective of what is unique and special in humans, namely, our capacity and desire to make up our own lives. However, for this to be true, another assumption is required, namely, that the process of choosing means that would coincide with certain aims or advance certain preferences is a clean, reasonable process by which an individual weighs a variety of options and picks the one most suitable to her goals. On this idealized description, which lies at the heart of a significant part of the liberal-democratic literature, Daniel Kahneman stated in his Nobel Prize acceptance speech that "rational models are psychologically unrealistic."[9]

The question of how the process of choosing occurs should be considered for the purpose of informing policies that respond to the normative demand for choice. Clearly, choice is bound by the context in which it occurs and is limited by the forms of rationality that the choosing individuals can utilize. Empirical research on choice exemplifies how a variety of elements, not commonly taken into account by liberal theories of autonomy and freedom, shape the way individuals make decisions and choices. Contemporary understanding of the processes of decision making as expressed in psychological studies and economic models is largely developed in the field of behavior economics, for which Kahneman and Tversky laid much of the groundwork.

Most prominently, the way choices are presented or framed, assumptions the individual makes about risk and potential gain, and marginal channel factors that make some options more accessible than others all have a decisive impact on the decision that is made. The heuristics of judgment demonstrate how choice acts rely primarily on intuition and other factors beyond a strict model of rational calculations of interest, or of matching means to aims.

In the 1970s, Kahneman and Tversky developed an innovative theory of cognitive processes, the two-system view that distinguishes intuition from reasoning and deliberative calculation. While their initial focus was on errors of intuition, the two-system view provides a broad base for the discussion of cognitive mechanisms in decision making. It is a descriptive analysis of the ways in which individuals access cognitive information in response to external stimuli such as a question or a need to make a decision. System 1, or the intuitive system, operates automatically and effortlessly. It is commonly not open to introspection, and its processes can take place in a parallel fashion while the individual thinks or does other things. It is an associative process that is quite resistant to change and intervention, and it is often emotionally charged. System 2, or the reasoning system, is slower, controlled, and rule-governed. It requires more effort, and thus is performed serially rather than in parallel. Because its processes are more accessible to introspection and because it is usually more affect-neutral, it is relatively more flexible and easier to modify through intervention, such as reasoning or amending the factual context of the decision.

The two-system view describes typical mental processes as they are expressed in ordinary life and as they can be measured in empirical experiments. It does not suggest a rigid distinction between the two systems; in fact, the suggestion has been made that prolonged practice can create high-level skills that would generate significant and accurate System 1 (or intuitive) responses to cognitive tasks, including those that before required the conscious effort of System 2 (reasoning). The chess player who needs but a quick look at the board before suggesting the winning move, and the nurse who detects signs of impending heart failure in a patient, to mention two famous examples, have practiced their professional skills enough to allow them to move from System 2 to System 1 and become habits of thought, which often produce trustworthy intuitive decisions.

Tversky and Kahneman further developed a broad theory of choice, related in particular to individuals' economic decisions. Prospect theory and its related notions of framing and heuristics of judgment present an understanding of the ways in which individuals weigh options and the processes they use to decide among them. This research has shown that framing, channel factors, over- and underrepresentation of extreme or familiar cases, and a host of other factors affect the outcome of choice problems, to the extent that several of the classic axioms of rational choice do not hold. As discussed in previous chapters, Tversky and Kahneman demonstrated systematic reversals of preference when the same problem is presented in different ways. Later studies have exemplified the effects of certain tendencies such as loss aversion and risk aversion (as opposed to gain seeking) on decisions in both lab experiments and realistic circumstances.

A key conclusion to draw from Kahneman and Tversky's work and the vast empirical literature in behavior economics and other fields that followed its inception is that rational choice is a notion that should be accepted only on highly qualified, or bounded, terms. In other words, the suggestion that people make personal decisions based on all available relevant information through rational calculations and in an autonomous fashion is true only if we offer complex qualifications to the term "rational." A variety of fields, including the theory of rational choice, were quick to adapt to this critique. In economic theory[10] as well as in disciplines where decision making is studied, such as social psychology,[11] business,[12] public health,[13] communications,[14] and neuroscience,[15] prospect theory and its consequences are today a main component of research on processes of decision making.

In the liberal theory of the state, however, this was not the case. Bounded rationality was not endorsed even in liberal theories about choice. It is not uncommon for scholars to discuss in unqualified terms the importance of an informed citizenry for the integrity and legitimacy of the political process. This line of argument fails to acknowledge the effects of the heuristics of judgment on the type of knowledge that citizens acquire from being exposed to the news, the structured choices that are provided to news consumers by editorial decisions about how to frame and present an issue, and the subsequent bounded rationality of citizens in decisions they make. Similarly, school choice advocates tend to ignore or downplay the complexities of the act of choice in its social context, including the strong impact of framing (or how choices are presented officially and unofficially) on the decisions individuals make. [16] More Choice for Parents was the slogan that summarized the political demand during the 2004 discussion of vouchers, thus sidestepping the question of what parents would do with this choice, these options, once they are made available.

Beyond the need to reconsider cognitive processes, the liberal-democratic debate on school choice could benefit from a closer look at the interpersonal and social processes that take place when choice, and school choice, are available.

How Families Choose a School

School choice designates a group of policies, all deploying the formal use of parental preferences in allocating children to schools. These policies aim to achieve a number of goals, some of them individual and some societal. Most significant among the aims related to individuals is the enhancement of parents' freedom and control over the education of their children. In the United States today, as in other countries, choice among schools is open to parents through two main avenues. First, they can choose whether to

129

send their children to a public or a private (parochial or other) school. If they choose the public system, they still face a residential choice: they can choose a school by choosing where to live, and thus which district and which neighborhood school, their children will be assigned to. Both of these options are dependent on the resources the family has available, and thus are open to some families but not to all. School choice programs that purport to include all families do so by providing either vouchers or similar mechanisms that allow all families to participate in the process, or that target families that lack resources in order to equalize their opportunities to choose. The effect of these programs varies.[17]

Beyond voucher systems, No Child Left Behind (NCLB) is another mechanism for choice, offering parents of children who are attending "failing" schools as defined by the law the opportunity to be reassigned. Recent reports suggest that the vast majority (up to 97 percent) of parents with children in failing schools choose to keep their children in those schools, even when it is their legal right to do otherwise.[18] At first glance, this decision seems unreasonable, and it clearly does not align with the intent of those who designed this policy. Some have suggested that districts discourage parents from using this choice option by framing it in ways that make it seem undesirable to parents, or by creating administrative hurdles for parents who wish to transfer their children (for example, by using incompatible registration dates).[19] This may be a significant part of the story, but it is not all of it. To understand the reasons for this and other choice behaviors, a closer look is needed into the actual process of choosing a school for one's child.

Consider a parent's choice of a school for her child. Assume that the child currently attends the local neighborhood school, which was deemed as failing under current NCLB standards. The parent can now choose among the failing school and three other schools in the area. One option is to choose intuitively, or based on highly accessible information that is incorporated into the parent's spontaneously available knowledge. "I don't mind that the school did not make AYP [Adequate Yearly Progress, as measured by raising the students' performance on state standardized tests as required by NCLB]," the parent might think. "I don't care too much about these titles. The school is close by and my child feels fine there. I am going to keep her there." Another parent might reach the opposite conclusion in a similarly intuitive fashion: "Finally," she might think, "a way out of the awful school where my child has been miserable for a number of years. I am definitely using this opportunity to opt out." Clearly, both parents are basing their spontaneous decisions on previously devised positions that rely on information they have acquired and processed over the years.

But this second parent's choice process does not end here. She now needs to choose among other available schools. If she knows and likes one of the other schools, for example, if she has a friend who has been sending her children there and has heard how happy they are, her decision is probably almost made. The availability of information on the second school through a social connection is a channel factor, or a marginal element that significantly increases the likelihood of a particular choice.

The reasons for either parent's choice vary, and they could be described through an agent-based or bounded rationality model as well as through a social and an institutional construction model. The two types of models illuminate different components of the barriers to parental choice, although some of the phenomena that they describe are similar.

A bounded rationality explanation of the barriers to utilizing parental choice opportunities might be related to reference dependence and loss aversion. The status quo bias[20] that influences various economic decisions exemplifies the loss-aversion tendencies, which can also explain some decisions in social areas outside the economic one. When presented with opportunities to change the status quo, individuals tend to calculate them not against end-state predictions or preferences but against the status quo, and potential losses tend to be magnified in their predictions while gains are trivialized or perceived as less significant. This tendency might account for the first parent's preference to remain in the failing school, based on what could be called "the devil I know" heuristics.

But there are other, mostly social, factors that come into play in the process of choosing a school. Interpretive and critical analyses of home-school relations show that "parental actions are not a matter of individual choice to be involved or not, but are indicative of long-standing cultural and institutional practices that give some people access to school resources while leaving others outside."[21] In a large sociological study of parental choice in the United Kingdom, the researchers report that respondents "talked of not enough choice and too much." The perception, particularly among more affluent parents, that they do not have enough choice was related to their sense that "schools were too much alike, or simply there were not enough schools available to choose from." Their sense that there was too much choice was mostly a result of the cost of information acquisition, and the burdens of acquiring and processing the many factors that seem relevant for the decision.[22]

While some studies suggest that the mere act of choice improves parental satisfaction,[23] possibly by increasing the investment of parents in the school, others show that the process of choosing is a cause for much anxiety. Parents strive to act as rational agents in the process of choosing a school for their children, but they usually feel that they fail. This failure leaves them with a sense of guilt, feeling as though they were not able to perform as good parents and to provide their children with the ideal choice.[24] "Here their failure to be rational, to be an ideal consumer, to live up to the expectations of the consuming subject embedded in guides and tables leaves them with a sense of not being good parents."[25]

The high cost of information acquisition, and the unfamiliarity of many parents with the details of the process, are possibly the most difficult aspects of school choice programs. Meira Levinson acknowledges these aspects when she requires, as part of her suggested "controlled choice" policy, that school choice programs en-list the help of an "energetic and effective system of school choice counseling at centers located in families' neighborhoods and open at times convenient for working parents."[26]

Such support in information gathering is significant to all parents; however, information acquisition can become prohibitive to parents who lack the needed social capital, the resources, the time, the connections or the language and cultural resources to effectively participate in what Lois André-Bechely calls "choice work"—the gathering of information, conducting conversations about schools, filling out forms, and following procedures. As one mother who forged documents to get her daughter into her middle school of choice confides, "I could have applied for open enrollment, but I don't know what that process is. If someone in the back room throws them up in the air and says, 'Hey, these people get in and those that don't, don't.' I don't know, you know, what that process is. Just like I don't know what the magnet process is. I don't understand that either, you know, so I didn't want to chance it."[27]

Thus, beyond individual differences and personal processes of decision making, social elements like language, class, and race can play a decisive role in the accessibility of school choice. With the changing landscape of successful and failing schools, "the resources necessary for making informed choices about schools are not available for many parents. Given the overwhelming number of working and single mothers in urban public school districts and realizing that choice work is added to the women's work that mothers already do on behalf of their children's education, gender, race, and class relations all become important considerations for any analysis of parents' school choice practices."[28]

Beyond the lack of familiarity and the sense of alienation from educational institutions that being a minority (the mother quoted earlier is Hispanic) or an immigrant can create, the cost of acquiring all relevant information can create an impossible burden for parents:

[P]icture a densely formatted brochure sent home to parents with information ranging from a short statement about voluntary integration to a large section on how to qualify for a gifted magnet and four pages of magnet school names grouped by theme and listing only a phone number to call for more information. Picture this against the amount of work (as suggested in the brochure) parents should do when choosing among the various magnet schools: research schools, go on school tours, talk with other parents, talk with teachers, gather information needed to complete the application.[29]

The daunting task of deciphering the requirements and the educational and administrative lingo on the documents create multiple additional hurdles on the way to utilizing the choice system. Checking the wrong box may result in complete denial of one's application, as one mother in André-Bechely's study learned when she thought she was asking for transportation for her child but in fact checked a box that provided a release to the district to bus her child to any school in the district. Personal contact with administrators rarely makes choice easier, possibly because of the high volume of requests they handle. One mother said, "They're not letting me have access to the information to get my foot in the door or to get my child's foot in the door so to speak."[30]

Some researchers have suggested that parents construct an understanding of the choice set available to them when choosing a school for their child in ways that do not always correspond with the choices formally offered. Differences are notable between racial and ethnic groups, and some studies have indicated a significant disparity among different racial groups' understanding of the choice set provided to them.[31] One study indicated that urban parents tend to believe that if they send their children to suburban schools, they will do better academically, and assume that the particular school they choose does not matter much.[32] The low-income, urban, mostly minority parents in this study did not consider specific educational offerings of different schools, but rather relied on anecdotal information (or channel factors) and perceived social status of the school in their decision. The information available to them, as well as their access to information about the school, was greatly limited by their location and social positioning. Race and class have an important impact not only on the accessibility of schools and administrators, and on parents' understanding of choice sets, but also on the networks available to them to support the gathering of information on schools. Studies of social networks and their use in making information accessible to parents have found that "[h]igher socioeconomic status individuals are more likely to have higher quality education networks. Education networks also exhibit a high degree of racial segregation."[33] Because networks can reduce the cost of information gathering and make data about available schools and their desirability more accessible, [34] the quality of one's network is material to the quality of the decision made. The stratification of social networks exacerbates race and class differences, further disadvantaging lower socioeconomic status (SES), minority, and immigrant parents who are trying to choose good schools for their children.

Implications for School Choice Policy

As demonstrated by the preceding sections, policies designed to offer choice to parents in the schooling of their children should be informed by actual processes of choice making by individuals and families, as well as by the educational and social aims they wish to promote. Recent studies that look carefully at the ways parents use choice opportunities point to the same conclusion, namely, that the details of actual choice processes must inform choice policies in a more elaborate way.[35] If choice policies are not solely aimed at introducing the market logic into the provision of education, but also at equalizing access and opportunity, realizing the promise of freedom or other ideals attached to choice, a simple laissez-faire approach will not do.[36] The structure of choice policies in schooling should take into account the actual limitations and challenges parents and families face in making these choices, in addition to specifying the aims of the policy and addressing them in the policy design.

Some critics have suggested that the privatization (or marketization) of a public good, like education, would generate an unequal distribution building on existing inequalities in society. Some of the studies discussed here have offered a detailed account of the ways in which this unequal distribution of education occurs through the mechanism of choice. This is important as a response to some egalitarian suggestions such as Brighouse's that school choice programs do not hinder social justice. While school choice may not necessarily impede social justice, in effect it often does. While this does not mean that choice needs to be abandoned, as Brighouse too argues, it does mean that it needs to be amended. Merely presenting individuals with choice does not enhance their freedom, nor does it increase their opportunities to pursue their preferences. Choice does not enhance social equality or justice in all cases, and it does not in itself promote any of the goods that liberals, libertarians, or egalitarians espouse and aspire for.

All this does not need to be perceived as a precursor to a suggestion that the state rather than the parents must make the decisions about children's schooling. Structured paternalism maintains a significant role for the state, but it does so as a way to support individual choice and enhance the opportunities available to all individuals. The discussion on the limits of school choice and the boundaries to implementing choice policies equitably can support an argument for redesigning choice policies in ways that maintain the dual aims of choice in education, both as a private good meant to enhance freedom and opportunity and as a public good meant to enhance social justice and civic equality.

By way of conclusion, I point out two main areas in which structured paternalist policies can be productively developed— policies that organize choice sets and support individuals in the process of choosing based on the motivation to advance their interests, needs, and preferences. The first has to do with the ways in which choices are communicated to the public. The second has to do with the equitable design of the choice set.

First, in response to the existing understanding of cognitive and social processes of choosing, public institutions in charge of enabling school choice (state and federal governments as well as school districts) need to pay close attention to minimizing the cost of information acquisition. The burden of choice policies on the choosing individual undermines some of the potential private advantages of choice, and inasmuch as the choice policy has aims related to education as a private good, it should find ways to relieve some these burdens. In addition, because the costs of information acquisition are not equally distributed across social groups, and tend to be higher for those who already have fewer resources, public institutions should put additional emphasis on supporting disadvantaged families.

The ways in which individuals choose should inform the design of policies, including the way they are communicated to the public. Particular emphasis should be put on the framing of options and the potential influence of channel factors on the actual accessibility of choices. For example, when developing a program like the one that allows parents to opt out of a failing school under NCLB, it is important to take into account a number of related considerations. The public presentation of the opportunity to choose, the framing of the different options, and the accessibility of assistance in the process are crucial elements to the success of such programs. An evaluation of the degree of participation and the reasons for individuals to choose whether to participate is important for the ongoing restructuring of public campaigns and other forms of presentation. A focus on information reflects an acknowledgment of individual practices of choice making, as well as the need to equalize access to information as a way to support individuals from all backgrounds in the process of choosing a school. Class, race, and language barriers that support some parents' involvement while minimizing others' access to their children's schools are ever present in the processes of choosing a school. One main lesson is that a real opportunity to take advantage of choice policies relies considerably on the accessibility of information. This suggestion carries significant implications for policy making.

The crucial role of accessible information to the success of school choice programs is acknowledged in some studies. As Brighouse suggests, "Parents in the U.S. studies have no comparable data on which to base their choices . . . with that data they would be significantly empowered to choose well. . . . Poor choosing should be relegated to a problem at the margins of the system with sufficiently aggressive regulation of, and public education about, choice."[37] Poor choosing is assumed by many scholars to exist mostly among poor parents (this is true in the context of school choice, but not only there). Herbert Gintis goes as far as suggesting that guardians should be appointed to children whose parents are particularly poor choosers.[38] But the studies just discussed suggest that poor choosing is widespread enough to deem the concerns about poor choosing misplaced. Appointing guardians to children whose parents cannot choose well would require an external evaluation of capabilities, which would undermine much of the deregulatory effects that some choice policies set out to achieve (not to mention the grave potential for overintervention and class-based discrimination). Brighouse's suggestion that parents need more comparable data does not address many parents' sense in the NCLB era that the amount of information they need to wade through is impossible to decipher or navigate. Making decisions based on these abundant data is still difficult for many parents, and not only the poor among them. Still, I agree with Brighouse's conclusion that sufficient regulation of and education about choice can support most parents through the process, until a desirable decision is reached. This suggestion is based on the assumption that stands at the core of this book: that choice should be structured so as to enhance not only individual opportunity but also social goals, civic equality being primary among them.

For school choice to fulfill its promises, a greater public and educational focus on choice making could provide important tools to individuals as they face their choice sets. The studies of actual choices and how they are made point to the need to present choices through public campaigns in ways that make them available and accessible to individuals as they weigh their options. It is important to educate children and adults to be literate in the processes of choosing, but it is equally important to create and present choice sets in ways that acknowledge the challenges present in the process of choice and their effects on the decisions made.

Making information more accessible not only reduces the cost of its acquisition, but also supports the development of relevant skills that improve the quality of the decision-making process. Because intuition has been shown to have a decisive role in a significant portion of choice acts, and because intuition is defined as judgment based on accessible information and perception, affecting choice processes requires a consideration of System 1 or intuitive perception. The most influential way to facilitate reasonable choice making is not by facilitating autonomy or critical reflection, but rather through finding ways to make relevant data more accessible to individuals at the moment of choice, thus making an intuitive decision more reasonable as it relies more significantly on relevant information rather than on channel factors, misguided information, and mistaken intuitions.

The design of policies that can support individuals in making decisions and choices in a variety of personal, social, and political contexts should aim at affecting highly accessible or intuitive processes and not solely informing the processes that take place consciously and slowly. To go back to prospect theory's language, to influence the way choices are made, one must inform System 1 and not solely System 2 processes.

When making information accessible to choosing families, more than quantitative measures of universal success should be provided. While the rate of success of current students in standardized tests has become the norm of accountability, the knowledge a parent can glean from these percentages is minimal. It is also not always relevant for the decision about each parent's particular child. The question of school accountability regarding making its students proficient in reading or math may be important to taxpayers, so they can assess how their school taxes are put to use. But there is much more, and different, information a parent needs in order to make an informed decision about what school her child will attend, with her abilities, preferences, needs, and aspirations. This information has to be available and organized in ways that make it accessible to choosing families.

Informing families of their choice set is essential enough to the success of a choice program that far more attention should be given to its detail in both scholarly debate and public discourse, as well as in policy making. Several steps can be taken to ensure that information acquisition does not become a prohibitive aspect of the policy, and that it does not divide the more affluent and the more involved from the less so. Because social capital and level of involvement are strong indicators of the quality of one's network, and because different groups of parents tend to rely variably on more or less formal sources of information, policy makers can positively affect equal accessibility of information on schools for all parents. For example, in order to equalize the access of information for those whose social networks are less effective (i.e., those that yield less information, or yield information of lower quality, or those that require further effort), policy makers can provide information centers that would be accessible to those who need them. Official advice as well as opportunities to network can be provided through such neighborhood resource and information centers. In addition, network studies have shown the importance of informal information gathering for decision making in school choice (and other choice) contexts. To support these processes for those who have fewer effective networks, local education authorities can rely on various community leaders (or "mavens") to communicate information about schools and options, and to support the generation of more effective networks through these key individuals—religious leaders, local school staff, and other well-situated individuals. This form of structured paternalist policy making, which promotes social goals while keeping in mind the needs and preferences of individuals, is a justified form of intervention.

The flow of information is thus an important aspect for scholars and policy makers to consider if choice programs are to fulfill some of their promises, justice and equality, cost effectiveness and freedom. But to make any of these promises more likely to be fulfilled, a vital first step is to consider the structure of the choice set itself. This chapter focuses on improving the opportunities to choose; it thus gives only cursory attention to questions of provision. This area is clearly of great importance in the discussion, as the availability of desirable options to choose among is a key aspect of choice policies. One of the main conclusions in this area would relate to the need to create a greater diversity among schools, so that they are not all judged on one scale of performance, but provide unique opportunities and substantive choices to the diverse student population that attends them, both among and (even more significantly) within schools. [39] The construction of the choice set must take into account basic values and visions that the state espouses—for example, the advancement of science or the arts—as well as local preferences such as specific cultural values. Choice sets of schools must not be differentiated along quality lines, as they often are today. The choice between a failing school and a successful school is not a choice of the kind a liberal-democratic state should offer its members, as this kind of choice stands to perpetuate social fissures rather than promote civic equality and personal freedom. A reasonably diverse choice set would include schools that are differentiated along lines other than mere quality, and which provide different paths (vocational or academic), different content foci (art, humanities, sports, computer science), different pedagogic approaches (open, structured, child-centered), or different institutional structures (brick and mortar, online). In countries where the separation of church and state does not confine the public education system as it does in the United States, schools that belong to different denominations can be added to the list.

These options can all be equally good, but they match different interests, styles, preferences, and identities. The differentiation in these areas is wide-ranging, and the opportunity for free expression of familial and personal styles is important for the well-being of individuals and for the preservation of diversity within society, as well as for considerations of equality and fairness.

The act of choice itself can produce in this context an advantage for those who choose. Some studies have shown that parents who choose are more satisfied than those who were not assigned to choice programs, as well as more satisfied than parents who were assigned to those programs but chose not to participate. Both of these groups of less-satisfied parents sent their children to a default school, usually the neighborhood school. Other studies indicate that the act of choosing, and the "choice work" that it entails, are evidence that the child has a more involved parent, which in turn is a positive factor in the academic success of the child. The causal relation here is unclear (possibly the parents were involved and therefore participated in the choice program, rather than vice versa). But apparently the personal, cognitive, familial, and social processes required to choose a school contribute something to the expression of parental involvement.

Consequently, if they are to be present within a given educational system, choice programs at their best should be structured so as to require all families to choose rather than targeting only some of them. Eliminating the default option in this case is an important step toward making choice fulfill the promises of equality and fairness. When all families are involved in choosing a school, some of the problems of choice programs disappear. The tendency of these programs to separate rich from poor, as in some of the instances of choice between public and private, and the choice among areas of residence, is eliminated. So is the problem of separating the poor from the very poor, or the poor and engaged from the poor and disengaged, as is sometimes the case with optional choice programs for lower-income families. The effect of "creaming" everyone who has resources—material or otherwise—from neighborhood schools, an effect that leaves those schools poorer in resources and community involvement, is much reduced when choice is mandatory. When everyone chooses, the act of choice does not generate or indicate greater social capital. With proper support, the process of choosing is less burdensome, and its consequences more favorable to the participants.

In areas where decisions are made solely in a personal manner, such as in the context of intimate relations, paternalist intervention may be required to avoid destructive choices. But in the area of school choice, where the decision is among structured institutional options, destructive choices can for the most part be eliminated from the choice set by the state. When only acceptable choices are available to families, the challenge that remains is how to support them in choosing what is good for their child. In education, as in some of the areas discussed in previous chapters, there is no correct choice to which all reasonable agents should adhere. Thus, significant attention should be given to the construction of a diverse and helpful choice set as well as to the proper presentation of its content.

The careful construction and communication of a choice set for families to respond to is a form of structured paternalism. The state provides education, and it thus constructs the choice set available to families. Even if the state were to abandon the idea of public provision of education, it would most likely still be responsible for regulating and supervising private providers, thus still contributing significantly to the construction of the choice set. Structured paternalism is inevitable here as in some other areas, and utilizing this approach to social policy making can increase the opportunities available to individuals and express respect to their equal standing as members of a democratic society. By constructing the choice set and properly communicating it, the state shares with families the responsibility for the consequences of the decisions they make.

—⁓— Conclusion —⁓—

STRUCTURED PATERNALISM AND THE LANDSCAPE OF CHOICE

CHOICE IS ONE OF THE GREATEST PROMISES of democratic social life today. Contrary to polities and eras where individuals were strapped to preexisting social structures, unable to overcome the path that was laid for them by the lottery of history and luck, members of liberal democracies today face a lifetime of choices. An individual is invited to make her voice heard through her choices, and to validate through personal expression the identity she espouses. In personal matters related to sexuality, religion, culture, parenting, and family life, choice is perceived as essential, affirming the individual's uniqueness. The liberal-democratic political and social ethos assumes that the revisability of preferences is an important aspect of freedom, and thus the ongoing process of choice and expression forms a key aspect of the democratic vision. When properly construed, choice can allow for the expression and affirmation of one's preferences, values, and affiliations. Starting from this perspective, this book offers an argument for structuring social policies that would allow for choice to fulfill its promise.

Paternalism

For choice to live up to the ideals of freedom, civic equality, justice, and equal well-being, policies of choice have to be designed with

144

these ideals at their core, while keeping in mind the realities of human experience in its diversity. If individuals are to choose in ways that are conducive to liberal-democratic ideals, their choice sets have to be reasonably structured, and the options offered to them should be conveyed in accessible and helpful forms. In other words, paternalist thought has to be put into the design of choice policies, meaning that policy makers must keep in mind what is good for members of the relevant constituency when they design policies that invite choice. For policy makers to think about what is "good for you" when they design these policies should not be perceived as a demeaning motivation, but rather as a way to realize the ideal of the state as being of service to its public, striving to realize the promise of civic equality and personal freedom.

Rights provide the first line of defense in a democracy against harms that individuals can cause each other, as well as against harms that institutions can cause to individuals. Both adults and children are protected by an array of rights that organize the landscape of choices they can make; structured paternalism provides the next layer of social policy aimed at advancing individual well-being and civic equality. Paternalism in the construction of choice sets makes sense in some areas, particularly those related to consumption and certain economic activities, where paternalist policies can advance choices that society endorses. In these areas, where we have expert opinions that can often be trusted, and where most individuals would do well if they trusted expert opinion, there is room for instituting default rules and other paternalist mechanisms that would support individual well-being.

In other areas, however, default rules and the reliance on expert opinion make little sense. Broadly speaking, choices that are intimately linked to personal expression of identity, to traditions and value sets, to intimate and familial relations, are less suitable for formal mechanisms such as default rules. Expert opinions matter only marginally in these contexts. The way to express structured paternalism in intimate and identity-related areas, such as sexuality, cultural affiliation, and domestic relations, is through the introduction of support mechanisms that help avoid destructive choices and provide opportunities for self-expression. For example, by providing structured ways out of relations and affiliations—domestic or cultural—which an individual may reject, the state can support the well-being and opportunities of all members without intervening in their freedom to make choices about their lives.

For choice to fulfill its promise, it is important to clearly distinguish choice from freedom. Sometimes choice can effectively be equated with freedom, but many other times choice is hindered by freedom, and freedom can be undermined by the existence of choice. Most of the cases considered in this book have to do with these areas where choice as a route to freedom does not always make sense as a policy. Belonging to a religion or a culture, choosing a spouse, maintaining intimate relations, and educating children are all areas where the expression of one's preferences is important to almost all individuals. Thinking about these cases solely as instances of choice does not always capture the essence of the proper relations between the state and the individual in these domains. Nor does it always maintain or enhance individual freedom.

In these areas, there is more room for eliminating destructive or severely undesirable options from one's choice set than for carefully structuring a choice set of potential spouses, available religions, or possible cultures to choose from. The elimination of destructive choices can often be achieved in these areas by providing better, more desirable, or less destructive options and supporting individuals as they embark on the process of expressing their identities or preferences in these more desirable ways. Providing entrance paths to members of minority cultures who are oppressed or who subjectively do not belong to their cultures of origin is an important way of expanding opportunities without focusing on choice as the organizing policy for cultural belonging and accommodation.

In the mixed context of parenting and public education, providing a broad and diverse array of schooling options and supporting parents in finding their way among these options is another way of allowing for personal preferences and identities to be expressed in the public domain, and in the intimate domain of parenting. In these areas, the logic of choice requires freedom as well as intervention and support; it requires an adherence to a set of values that favors individual well-being over shared group preferences. Most important, it takes choice for what it is—a diverse tool that can serve various purposes, from equality to freedom, and should thus be structured with detailed consideration of its impact on the individuals on which it is imposed.

Opportunities

The elimination of destructive choices and the careful construction of choice sets are vital for the expansion of individual opportunities. The expansion of opportunities is made possible when individuals face a choice set that is well-structured, and which provides diverse, desirable options that can potentially enhance the well-being of the choosing individuals. Those individuals need not be autonomous in any strict sense. But they should have developed some cognitive and other tools that would enable them to go through a productive process of choice. Policies should not assume that all individuals or all adults possess these tools. Rather, they should consider how the policy can be designed so as to respond to the choosing capacities of the constituency it addresses.

The state can support the development of appropriate choice capacities through formal education, but it can also contribute to the productive implementation of these capacities through properly designing choice sets, framing choices accessibly and helpfully, and providing needed support mechanisms to individuals who are facing choices. The construction of the context of choice is important, and it changes from choices that take place in daily situations, such as selecting a health plan, to choices that occur at critical junctions of an individual's life.

Some of these critical choices were discussed here—the choices of women in the context of a complicated pregnancy or an abusive relationship, as well as the decision to leave one's culture. The expansion of opportunities is far from analogous to the expansion of the choice set, particularly in these critical cases. As mentioned, in the context of destructive choices or of choices that expert opinion, when it is relevant, would identify as utterly undesirable, the expansion of opportunities would be tied to the elimination of those choices, and thus the narrowing down of the choice set. A narrowed-down choice set can be effective in other circumstances as well. Thinking back on the case of school choice, offering parents the choice among hundreds of schools can often be more confusing and exasperating than empowering or liberating. It can further disadvantage parents who have fewer networks, knowledge, and resources to consider and weigh these options. In this way, a wider choice set would undermine the well-being of some children and the civic equality of their families.

Alternatively, a choice set can be constructed after identifying the most important elements to the relevant constituency—in the context of school choice, for example, pedagogic styles or curricular foci or vocational opportunities. Providing a well-structured choice set both within and among the local schools would in this case provide greater opportunities, understood as the possibility to enhance one's well-being through choice or the expression of preferences. It would also support equality by minimizing the costs of using the opportunity to choose, as well as support the freedom individuals have to school their children according to their values and preferences.

Education

Education played an important role throughout the discussion, and it should be considered in detail by anyone who is interested in the role of choice in democratic life. The role of education in realizing the promise of choice is twofold. First, education is a process by which individuals learn to identify and develop their preferences, and learn to relate those preferences to others and express them through choosing one course, path, or option over others. Second, education is effectively provided by the state through the institutional structure of schools, and the public debate on the organization, ethos, and content of education in schools testifies to their importance as public expressions of value choices. In other words, schools both form and communicate identities, and hence the significance of carefully designing them and the choices within and among them. In the current context, making sure that schools teach the practice of choice, that they provide choice on an ongoing basis and not merely as a onetime act of choosing a school, and that they allow for the expression of choices after those are made, are all imperative to realizing choice in a democratic society.

Outside the compulsory education system, investing in adult education is an important way for society to express its support for the value of choice. Adult education was discussed here in the context of the choice to exit a comprehensive cultural group, and as part of the price society should be willing to share with the exiting individual. Adult education in this case is a pathway into another cultural context, an opportunity to expand one's options for employment, creating new social ties and developing social capital that was not available for her in this form before. In other circumstances, adult education (including both general and vocational education) can serve as an important way to expand individuals' opportunities in ways that, while they can sometimes be paternalist, do not restrict freedom or infantilize. The democratic state should invest in lifelong learning, or the education of adult members, because it stands out as a vital way of investing in both individual freedom and civic equality, and because it signifies a commitment to providing choices for individuals that allow them to develop and express their vision of the good life.

How Choice Can Fulfill Its Promise

Too often in theoretical studies of choice, the tendency is to assume that individuals are rational, autonomous, and able to choose, simply because they are adults. Sometimes reference is made to the need to develop autonomy or rationality, or other capacities required for choosing, usually through schools. One concern that this latter approach should raise is that it allows for the theory to continue to rely on the assumption that all adults are formally autonomous because they participated in autonomy-facilitating education, or that they are all rational because they are, for the most part, graduates of the schooling system. Political structures can thus continue to rely on the presumed autonomy and rationality of individuals when making recommendations for desirable forms of policy making.

Bringing studies about actual processes that individuals go through when they face choices into the theoretical and political debate should alter this common framework. Empirical studies about choice, coming from behavioral economics, network studies, ethnographic research, and other methodologies should inform democratic theories of regulation and choice and the policies they develop, and should direct them to pay closer attention to the challenges of implementing some of the theoretical ideals in the social world. These challenges do not call for abandoning the commitment to equality or freedom, or to other key ideals of liberal-democratic theory. Rather, they should direct some of the conversation toward searching for practical ways to realize these ideals, to achieve the goals of a freer, more equal society, and to move theory and social reality closer together. Policies based on this closer connection can work toward a society where more individuals can exercise greater power over their lives and enjoy greater opportunities to improve their well-being and to express their preferences and identities. Policies that aim to achieve these goals, that aim to make what is "good for you" available within the set of options one can choose from, can be perceived as desirable from a variety of liberal, libertarian, communitarian, and egalitarian perspectives.

Throughout the history of choice in political thought, it has been paired with responsibility. Choice implies responsibility—it suggests that an individual is capable of taking one path over another for some reason, and that the consequences of this action, this decision, are for her to bear. Desirable forms of paternalism offer an opportunity to share this responsibility between the individual and the state. Why is a shared responsibility justified? The reason is that while Oliver Twist and Mr. Darcy are long gone from today's democratic societies, one's circumstances of birth still affect her possibilities, opportunities, and options.[1] The choice set each member of society faces is more varied than the one available centuries ago, but it is still not equal across classes, genders, and abilities. An individual is free to attempt to write her own life story, but the conditions offered to her by her morally arbitrary traits, by the lottery of history and biology that brought her to be herself, are important factors in her ability to realize her dreams, or even to dream them.

The state thus has a moral obligation to share with the individual the responsibility for the consequences of the choices she took. To fulfill this moral obligation, the state should have an explicit and structured role in generating the individual's choice set, and in directing her at the very least to avoid the most destructive choices possible. Individuals make choices in all circumstances—Oliver Twist chooses to defy the rules in his orphanage, and keeps some of his independence of mind and action throughout his ordeal; Jane Austen's Mr. Darcy decides to persistently court Elizabeth after she rejects him. But the context in which they choose is severely narrowed down by the circumstances of their birth. In a contemporary democratic society that prides itself on the opportunities it provides to all its members, opportunities to pursue their dreams and to transcend the circumstances of their birth, choice is ever more important as a guideline to social policies. The ideal of choice must be augmented by an understanding of the social realities in which it operates, including challenges of cognitive makeup and social positioning. Constructed in response to both values and social realities, the practice of choice can provide expanded opportunities to all individuals and support them in becoming civic equals and enjoying the well-being that a democratic society can offer.

NOTES

Chapter 1
To Choose or Not to Choose?

1. Some of the literature refers to "architecture of choice" in this context; I prefer talking about the landscape of choice because I see this process as gradual, and organic to the evolvement of social practices, rather than fully orchestrated and planned as the term "architecture" seems to me to indicate.

2. This definition or depiction resonates with the capabilities approach, which describes capabilities as a practical choice to function, or having a substantive freedom in areas that people have reason to value. While the focus on choice here is indeed reminiscent of Amartya Sen and Martha Nussbaum's, I do not explore the dimensions of individual life and social functioning in which more choice is clearly advisable. Rather, my concern is the structure of policies that would best provide opportunities to individuals, and particularly to the ways in which personal preferences affect and are affected by the landscape of choice that these policies generate. This mutual influence stands at the core of the current investigation of choice as a normative policy guideline.

See, for example, Amartya Sen, "Capability and Well-Being," in *The Quality of Life*, ed. Martha Nussbaum and Amartya Sen (Oxford: Clarendon Press, 1993), 30–53; Martha Nussbaum, *Frontiers of Justice* (Cambridge, MA: Harvard University Press, 2006).

3. See a comparative study suggesting that "while differences in other determinants of organ donation explain much of the variation in donation rates, after controlling for those determinants presumed consent legislation has a positive and sizeable effect on organ donation rates." Alberto Abadie and Sebastian Gay, "The Impact of Presumed Consent Legislation

on Cadaveric Organ Donation: A Cross-Country Study," *Journal of Health Economics* 25, no. 4 (July 2006): 599–620.

4. For this reason, Richard Thaler and Cass Sunstein consider default rules to be a libertarian form of regulation. I consider it to be compatible with liberal values as well, and develop this argument in the next chapter. Richard A. Thaler and Cass R. Sunstein, "Libertarian Paternalism," *American Economic Review* 93, no. 2 (May 2003): 175–79.

5. Isaiah Berlin, introduction to *Five Essays on Liberty*, ed. Henry Hardy (Oxford: Oxford University Press, 2002), 51–52.

Chapter 2
Why Paternalism Is Good for You

1. Seana Shiffrin suggests that we need to understand "why paternalism is important" when we embark upon a debate about its permissibility. Seana Valentine Shiffrin, "Paternalism, Unconscionability Doctrine, and Accommodation," *Philosophy and Public Affairs* 29 (2000): 205–50, at 205. In this chapter, I consider why paternalism is important for democratic theory.

2. Joel Feinberg, "Legal Paternalism," in *Rights, Justice, and the Bounds of Liberty* (Princeton, NJ: Princeton University Press, 1980), 111 n. 2.

3. For a discussion of the challenges to civic equality in education, and in particular the view that "a certain type of equality—civic equality—is actually internal to the idea of educational adequacy for a democratic society," see Debra Satz, "Equality, Adequacy and Education for Citizenship," *Ethics* 117 (July 2007): 623–48, at 623.

4. Berlin, introduction to *Five Essays on Liberty*, 53–54.

5. Gerald Dworkin, "Paternalism," *The Monist* 56 (1972): 64–84, reprinted in Rolf Sartorius, ed., *Paternalism* (Minneapolis: University of Minnesota Press, 1983), 19–34, and again more recently in Gerald Dworkin, ed., *Mill's* On Liberty: *Critical Essays* (Rowman and Littlefield, 1997), 61–82.

6. Sartorius, *Paternalism*, 20.

7. Bernard Gert and Charles Culver, "Paternalistic Behavior," *Philosophy and Public Affairs* 6 (1976): 45–58.

8. Gerald Dworkin, "Paternalism: Some Second Thoughts," in Sartorius, *Paternalism*, 105–11, at 107. I return to autonomy and the debate over the distinction between children and adults later.

9. Thaler and Sunstein, "Libertarian Paternalism," 175–79, at 175.

10. This is a main design that Sunstein and Thaler support, as mentioned in their introduction. They suggest that if employers establish de-

fault deductions for savings, for example, more employees will choose this default option and increase their levels of savings. Freedom of choice is maintained, and coercion is avoided or minimized, by giving those who so choose the opportunity to opt out of the default policy.

11. Thaler and Sunstein, "Libertarian Paternalism," 177.

12. Robert Nozick *Anarchy, State and Utopia* (New York: Basic Books, 1994).

13. Herbert Morris, "A Paternalistic Theory of Punishment," in *A Reader on Punishment*, ed. Antony Duff and David Garland (Oxford: Oxford University Press, 1994), 96. Quoted and discussed in David J. Garren, "Paternalism, Part I," *Philosophical Books* 47, no. 4 (October 2006): 334–41. For a review of Morris's perspective, see David Dolinko, "Morris on Paternalism and Punishment," *Law and Philosophy* 18 (1999): 345–61. On the adult-children context of paternalism, see Marion Smiley, "Paternalism and Democracy," *Journal of Value Inquiry* 23 (1989): 299–318.

14. For a Kantian discussion along these lines, see Tamar Schapiro, "What Is a Child?" *Ethics* 109 (July 1999): 715–38.

15. Some of these protections are based on physical development—driving, for example. Others are related to the combination of physical and mental development, like sexual conduct. Contract laws and employment regulation are mostly meant to protect children against exploitation, again because of the assumption that they cannot fend for themselves.

16. Chapter 4 expands on many of the points in this paragraph.

17. Peter de Marneffe, "Avoiding Paternalism," *Philosophy and Public Affairs* 34, no. 1 (2006): 68–94, at 68.

18. Cass R. Sunstein and Richard H. Thaler, "Libertarian Paternalism Is Not an Oxymoron" (working paper, AEI-Brookings, 2003).

19. Sunstein and Thaler favor paternalistic policies that improve individual well-being beyond what those individuals can achieve when they rely solely on their imperfect processes of decision making. They suggest that libertarians should support those policies which maintain as much freedom of choice as possible out of respect for individual autonomy. In other words, policies in areas such as saving or health care should structure the choices available to individuals in the least interventionist way, encouraging individuals to make as free and rational decisions as possible, and maintain structural freedom through opt-out and other mechanisms.

20. Chapter 6 expands the discussion of their work and suggest additional effects it should have on choice policies.

21. B. J. McNeil, S. G. Pauker, H. C. Sox, and A. Tversky, "On the Elicitation of Preferences for Alternative Therapies," *New England Journal of Medicine* 306 (1982): 910–24.

22. Vilfredo Pareto, *Manual of Political Economy* (New York: Augustus M. Kelly, 1971), 103.

23. Dan Ariely, *Predictably Irrational* (New York: HarperCollins, 2008).

24. Even if paternalism is justified on normative terms, some may argue that it has no room in policy making because of its inefficiency. The question of efficiency originates from the rationality assumption in economics, where it is at least as pronounced as in the political-philosophical literature. The rationality assumption in its thin or minimal form suggests that rational individuals seek to maximize profit, or that rational individuals seek an alignment of their means to their ends. Assuming descriptive rationality is a common starting point for economic analysis, offering a metric for examining the effects of individuals' expressed preferences and actions on the behavior of market models and weighing the outcomes of their choices. The recognition that systematic "errors" or deviations from this basic understanding of rationality is becoming more widespread in the field of economics, with empirical evidence accumulating to indicate that individuals tend to be afflicted by a host of biases when making decisions that could ideally be computed by simple rational methods.

Consequently, some authors suggest that in order to protect efficiency, it is necessary to compensate for these biases or deviations from standard understandings of rationality by implementing paternalistic policies. See, for example, Christine Jolls and Cass R. Sunstein, "Debiasing through Law," *Journal of Legal Studies* 35 (2006): 199–242. Some studies analyze the efficiency of such paternalist policies and maintain that "paternalism is indeed compatible with the theoretical foundations of normative economics and, furthermore, that efficiency analysis provides a central justification for paternalism." See Eyal Zamir, "The Efficiency of Paternalism," *Virginia Law Review* 84, no. 2 (March 1998): 229–86. Other authors, however, reject paternalism as inefficient. They claim that while boundedly rational behavior does undermine individual utility maximization, the aggregate sum of decisions taken by boundedly rational individuals corrects itself to a point where there is no need to paternalistically correct it through external regulation. (See Nathan Berg and Gert Gigerenzer, "Psychology Implies Paternalism? Bounded Rationality May Reduce the Rationale to Regulate Risk-Taking," *Social Choice Welfare* 28 [2007]: 337–59.)

In other words, Pareto maximization is possible even when individual-level deviations from classical rationality assumptions abound. However, even taking this latter counterargument into account, paternalism may still be justified from the perspective of the individual and her well-being. If legal regulation is needed to "de-bias" and correct deviations from desirable self-interested outcomes, the fact that Pareto optimization on a large scale is still possible does not salvage the individual from the damage her well-being or equal civic standing suffered because of her uninformed, misguided, or otherwise mistaken choices. Thus, both for efficiency's sake and for the sake of individual well-being, paternalism seems like a reasonable policy mechanism.

25. This pursuit can often be destructive to the individual herself, as the ongoing struggle over the paradigmatic issue of motorcycle helmets reveals. See the discussion in Marian Moser Jones and Ronald Bayer, "Paternalism and Its Discontents: Motorcycle Helmet Laws, Libertarian Values, and Public Health," *American Journal of Public Health* 97, no. 2 (February 2007): 208–17.

26. I focus on this question in chapter 6.

27. Judith R. Porter, Mary Summers, Suzanne Toton, and Hillary Aisenstein, "Service-Learning with a Food Stamp Enrollment Campaign: Community and Student Benefits," *Michigan Journal of Community Service Learning* 14, no. 2 (Spring 2008): 66–75.

28. Seana Valentine Shiffrin, "Paternalism, Unconscionability Doctrine, and Accommodation," *Philosophy and Public Affairs* 29 (2000): 205–50, at 207.

29. The description of paternalism as mostly motivational seems unsound in the area of policy making. Paternalism is not mainly motivational (as Dworkin's first argument suggests) or attributive (as his second one maintains). Paternalistic policies by and large are constructed around an account of public and individual welfare. A paternalistic policy would rarely be motivated exclusively by reasons of another individual's welfare. More often it would consider those alongside a vast array of other considerations and aims. Policies that are often used as clear examples of state paternalism, such as seat belts and motorcycle helmet laws, are often justified not only because they are protective of drivers and riders; other common justifications are the health care costs of injuries that are borne by society, or the discomfort of refusing to spend public funds on these expenses. Other justifications include insurance costs considerations, family members' preferences, and general views of just treatment in society. Thus, identifying paternalistic policy exclusively based on motivation does not seem to cover enough of the relevant policies.

30. The discussion in the next paragraphs focuses on Raz's views as presented in *The Morality of Freedom* (Oxford: Oxford University Press, 1986). His main arguments on paternalism are discussed in chapter 15 of that volume.

31. Raz, *Morality of Freedom*, 426.

32. Ibid., 427.

33. Ronald Dworkin, *Sovereign Virtue: The Theory and Practice of Equality* (Cambridge, MA: Harvard University Press, 2000), 217–18.

34. Raz, *Morality of Freedom*, 423. Raz also joins other liberals by sanctioning means-related paternalism as well as safety controls.

35. A different justification for assigning value to autonomy is its role in the project of legitimization. While the legitimacy of the state is of significance in a democracy, and the ability of citizens to give their informed consent to the laws that direct their lives seems to be a dividing line between authoritarian and democratic regimes, our knowledge of how individuals choose casts doubt on the value of referring to autonomy (and rationality) as necessary traits for this purpose. From studies on bounded rationality to contemporary studies that consider party affiliation as genetically based, autonomy does not seem to play an indispensable role in major political (and other) decisions we make. I cannot discuss here the effects of this suggestion on the project of legitimization, but simply point out that civic equality, which is one of the two main aims (along with individual well-being) of the current discussion, is a key condition of democratic legitimacy.

36. Dennis Thompson, *Political Ethics and Public Office* (Cambridge, MA: Harvard University Press, 1987), 154–55.

37. Joel Feinberg, *Harm to Self* (New York: Oxford University Press, 1986), 12.

38. Dworkin, *Sovereign Virtue*, 217–18. See discussion of some distinctions among these views in David J. Garren, "Paternalism, Part II," *Philosophical Books* 48, no. 1 (2006): 50–59.

39. Stephen Darwall, *Welfare and Rational Care* (Princeton, NJ: Princeton University Press, 2002).

Chapter 3
The Regulation of Intimacy

1. The seminal work on the topic is Susan Moller Okin's *Justice, Gender and the Family* (New York: Basic Books, 1989).

2. See exchange between Stephen Macedo and George Finnis in *Natural Law, Liberalism, and Morality*, ed. Robert P. George (Oxford: Clarendon Press, 1996).

3. Harry Kalven, "Privacy in the Tort Law—Were Warren and Brendeis Wrong?" *Law and Contemporary Problems* 31, no. 2 (Spring 1966): 327.

4. See a discussion of this point in Richard J. Arneson, "Egalitarian Jus-

tice versus the Right to Privacy," *Social Philosophy and Policy* 17, no. 2 (Summer 2000): 91–119.

5. Hannah Arendt, *The Human Condition* (Chicago: University of Chicago Press, 1998).

6. Seyla Benhabib offers a general account of these aspects of privacy in *Situating the Self* (London: Polity Press, 1992), esp. chap. 3.

7. The convergence between the conscience and the private is challenged by claims such as Amy Gutmann's, who in her *Identity in Democracy* (Princeton, NJ: Princeton University Press, 2003, chap. 4) advocates "two way protection" between church and state to allow for "a reciprocal relationship between ethical identity and democratic politics" and to further democratic justice. The justification of "non-interference by the political state in the free flow of commodity relations" as Benhabib puts it in *Situating the Self*, 108, may be the most stable matter within the private sphere, but these, as Arendt observed, are part of the "social" rather than public or political (and thus are not strictly a part of the private sphere). The economic aspects of one's conduct are commonly regulated by various state institutions. The household's privacy has been challenged by feminist authors (most notably Susan Moller Okin), who generally claim that in order to bring to light, and change, the gender power relations, the personal must be politicized. When the personal becomes political, it can no longer be intimate—for better or worse.

8. John Stuart Mill, *On Liberty* (Chicago: Henry Regnery, 1955), chap. 5, 85.

9. See a thorough discussion of the rise and fall of the harm principle as a judicial justification, substituting the claims from public morality, in Bernard E. Harcourt, "The Collapse of the Harm Principle," *Journal of Criminal Law and Criminology* 90, no. 1 (Fall 1999): 109–95.

10. As Arien Mack puts it in his editorial preface to an issue devoted to the question of privacy, *Social Research* 68, no. 1 (Spring 2001).

11. In the words of Anita Allen, who defines herself as one.

12. Samuel D. Warren and Louis D. Brendeis, "The Right to Privacy [The Implicit Made Explicit]," reprinted in Ferdinand David Schoeman, ed., *Philosophical Dimensions of Privacy: An Anthology* (New York: Cambridge University Press, 1984), 75–103.

13. Thomas Cooley, *Torts*, 2nd ed. (Chicago: Callaghan, 1888), 29.

14. Those are Thomas Scanlon's words in his response to Judith Jarvis Thomson, in an issue of *Philosophy and Public Affairs* dedicated to the right to privacy. Thomson herself argues against the right to privacy, claiming that it is a name for a cluster of rights that are generally derivative

of the rights to property and other personal rights. Judith Jarvis Thomson, "The Right to Privacy," Thomas Scanlon, "Thomson on Privacy," *Philosophy and Public Affairs* 4, no. 4 (Summer 1975): 295–314; 315–22.

15. Robert S. Gerstein, "Intimacy and Privacy," in Schoeman, *Philosophical Dimensions of Privacy*, 265–71.

16. Stanley I. Benn, "Privacy, Freedom and Respect for Persons," in Schoeman, *Philosophical Dimensions of Privacy*, 223–44.

17. Ruth Gavison, "Privacy and the Limits of Law," in Schoeman, *Philosophical Dimensions of Privacy*, 346–402.

18. *Planned Parenthood of Southeastern Pennsylvania v. Casey*, 505 U.S. 833 (1992). See a thorough analysis of Supreme Court decisions on abortion, planned parenthood, and other intimate issues in David J. Garrow, "Privacy and the American Constitution," *Social Research* 68, no. 1 (Spring 2001): 55–82.

19. Julie A. Mertus, "Beyond the Solitary Self: Voice, Community and Reproductive Freedom," *Columbia Journal of Gender and Law* 3, no. 1 (1992): 250.

20. Jean L. Cohen, *Regulating Intimacy* (Princeton, NJ: Princeton University Press, 2002), 20.

21. Ibid., 151.

22. Ibid., 178.

23. William E. Scheuerman, "Reflexive Law and the Challenges of Globalization," *Journal of Political Philosophy* 9, no. 1 (2001): 81–102, at 82.

24. Ibid., 84.

25. Cohen, *Regulating Intimacy*, 72.

26. Catherine Mackinnon, "Privacy v. Equality: Beyond Roe v. Wade," in *Feminism Unmodified* (Harvard, MA: Harvard University Press 1987); Carol Pateman, "Feminist Critiques of the Public/Private Dichotomy," in *Public and Private in Social Life,* ed. Stanley I. Benn and Gerald F. Gauss (New York: St. Martin's Press, 1983).

27. The quotes in this paragraph are all from Cohen's *Regulating Intimacy*, 66.

28. Ibid.

29. Beth Kyoko Jamieson, *Real Choices: Feminism, Freedom, and the Limits of Law* (University Park: Pennsylvania State University Press, 2001).

30. For a sensitive description of how abused women retain their autonomy, see Marilyn Friedman, *Autonomy, Gender and Politics* (New York: Oxford University Press, 2003).

31. Linda G. Mills, *Insult to Injury: Rethinking Our Responses to Intimate Abuse* (Princeton, NJ: Princeton University Press, 2006), 6.

32. Joseph Raz, "Liberty and Trust," in *Natural Law, Liberalism and*

Morality: Contemporary Essays, ed. Robert P. George (New York: Oxford University Press), 120.

33. The proliferation of cases in which older children—teenagers in some cases—were abandoned in hospitals and other facilities under the Safe Haven laws, often by poor parents or because their families could not bear the financial burden of their medical treatment, indicates that supports are required beyond the time of pregnancy. See *USA Today*, November 14, 2008, http://www.washingtontimes.com/news/2008/oct/14/vague-safe-haven-law-draws-out-of-state-cases/ (accessed March 10, 2009).

34. William Galston, *Liberal Purposes: Goods, Virtues, and Diversity in the Liberal State* (New York: Cambridge University Press, 1991).

35. See a critical discussion of the Western perspectives on clitoridectomy, including a claim that in effect it is commonly not hazardous to women's health or sexual pleasure, in Richard Shweder, "What about Female Genital Mutilation? And Why Understanding Culture Matters in the First Place," in *Engaging Cultural Differences: Multicultural Challenge in Liberal Democracies*, ed. Richard A. Shweder, Martha Minow, and Hazel R. Markus (New York: Russell Sage Foundation Press, 2002), 216–51.

36. For a discussion on the justification of this decision from a liberal-democratic perspective, comparing it to plastic surgery, see Amy Gutmann, *Identity in Democracy* (Princeton, NJ: Princeton University Press, 2003), 68–70.

37. See a comprehensive study of the innovative approach endorsed by drug courts and its consequences compared to the traditional criminal court approach, in James L. Nolan, *Reinventing Justice: The American Drug Court Movement* (Princeton, NJ: Princeton University Press, 2001). Nolan describes and critically discusses the supportive, individualized programs that these courts use, aimed at rehabilitating drug offenders. His measured discussion brings me to a conclusion that is more supportive of these courts than Nolan himself reaches. I share with Anita Allen the perspective that regards drug use as social rather than self-inflicted harm (see Anita L. Allen, *Why Privacy Isn't EVERYTHING* [Lanham, MD: Rowman and Littlefield, 2003]), and thus I believe that in this case too, prevention is far more ethically and practically warranted.

38. Certain criminologists, perhaps most notably John Braithwaite, have suggested that similar approaches should be applied to criminal behavior in other domains as well. These approaches aim to restore relations by supporting community involvement in the resolution after a crime has been committed, mandating compensation of the victim by the offender, and turning to punitive justice only when all else fails. John Braithwaite,

Restorative Justice and Responsive Regulation (New York: Oxford University Press, 2002).

Chapter 4
Paternalism toward Children

1. Developing the skills and habits of good citizenship is a justified role of the public education system. The focus here is on the basic protective structures required of institutions—like schools—that address children's needs. Beyond the requirements of structured paternalism, other goals can be developed, including those of citizenship education.

2. Ellen Key, *The Century of the Child* (New York: Knickerbocker Press, 1910).

3. Neil Postman, *The Disappearance of Childhood* (New York: Delacorte Press, 1982).

4. David Archard, *Children: Rights and Childhood* (London: Routledge, 1993).

5. F. Rothbaum, A. Grauer, and D. Rubin, "Becoming Sexual: Differences Between Child and Adult Sexuality," *Young Children* 52 (1997): 22–28.

6. A key study on contemporary comparative parenting practices is Annette Lareau, *Unequal Childhoods: Race, Class and Family Life* (Berkeley: University of California Press, 2003). Lareau describes the key correlations, and some of the underlying differences, among different class-based parenting styles:

Professionals' advice regarding the best way to raise children has changed regularly over the last two centuries. From strong opinions about the merits of bottle feeding, being stern with children, and utilizing physical punishment (with dire warnings of problematic outcomes should parents indulge children), there have been shifts to equally strongly worded recommendations about the benefits of breast feeding, displaying emotional warmth toward children, and using reasoning and negotiation as mechanisms of parental control. Middle-class parents appear to shift their behaviors in a variety of spheres more rapidly and more thoroughly than do working-class or poor parents.... Middle-class parents who comply with current professional standards and engage in a pattern of concerted cultivation deliberately try to stimulate their children's development and foster their cognitive and social skills. The commitment among working-class and poor families to provide comfort, food, shelter, and other basic support requires ongoing effort.... For working-class and poor families, sustaining children's natural growth is viewed as an accomplishment. (4–5).

Note that despite the clear differences, the commitment to provide for and protect children is evident in both styles of parenting, with both of them subscribing to the notion of childhood as deserving of sheltering and support.

7. Joel Feinberg, "A Child's Right to an Open Future," in Hugh La Folette and William Aiken, eds., *Whose Child? Children's Rights, Parental Authority and State Power* (Totowa, NJ: Rowman and Littlefield, 1980).

8. Henry Giroux, "Public Intellectuals and the Challenge of Children's Culture: Youth and the Politics of Innocence," *Review of Education / Pedagogy / Cultural Studies* 21, no. 3 (1999): 193–225.

9. Sue Malvern, "The Ends of Innocence: Modern Art and Modern Children," *Art History* 23, no. 4 (2000): 627–32.

10. Jean-Jacque Rousseau, *Emile or On Education*, trans. Barbara Foxley (London: Dutton, 1969).

11. Stephen Heath, "Childhood Times," *Critical Quarterly* 39 (1997): 16–27.

12. Roger Cox, *Shaping Childhood: Themes of Uncertainty in the History of Adult-Child Relationships* (New York: Routledge, 1996), 170.

13. Richard E. Farson, *Birthrights* (London: Collier Macmillan, 1974); John Holt, *Escape from Childhood* (Harmondsworth: Penguin, 1975).

14. Laura Purdy, *In Their Best Interest? The Case against Equal Rights for Children* (Ithaca, NY: Cornell University Press, 1992).

15. A. S. Neill, *Summerhill: A Radical Approach to Child Rearing* (New York: Hart Publications, 1960); Carl Rogers and L. Freiberg, *Freedom to Learn* (New York: Maxwell Macmillan International, 1994).

16. Others have argued for various distinctions within rights theories that can be applied more productively to children. For a valuable argument for preferring welfare rights over agency rights, see Harry Brighouse, "What Rights (If Any) Do Children Have?" in *The Moral and Political Status of Children*, ed. David Archard and Colin M. Macleod (New York: Oxford University Press, 2005), 31–52.

17. Onora O'Neill, "Children's Rights and Children's Lives," *Ethics* 98, no. 3 (1988): 445–63.

18. James Dwyer, "Changing the Conversation on Children's Education," in *Moral and Political Education*, Nomos XLIII, ed. Stephen Macedo and Yael Tamir (New York: New York University Press, 2002), 314–58.

19. Barbara Arneil, "Becoming versus Being: A Critical Analysis of the Child in Liberal Theory," in Archard and Macleod, *Moral and Political Status of Children*, 70–94. The current argument shares many of the critical

perspectives these three authors offer. My approach is probably closest to Arneil's, as she relies on children's dependence to develop her alternative view of childhood, based on the ethics of care. The current argument differs from this vision because a focus on vulnerability and subsequent forms of paternalism rather than on dependence puts more emphasis on protection than on relations. Consequently, I rely more on state institutions than Arneil's relational vision would favor.

20. Archard, *Children: Rights and Childhood*, 52.

21. O'Neill, "Children's Rights and Children's Lives," 445–63.

22. Christopher Jencks, *Childhood* (New York: Routledge, 1996), 2.

23. Jean Piaget, *The Child's Conception of the World* (New York: Harcourt, 1929).

24. J. Palmer, T. Smeeding, and B. Torrey Boyle, eds., *Vulnerable* (Washington, DC: Urban Institute Press, 1989).

25. John Locke, *Some Thoughts Concerning Human Understanding*, in *The Educational Writings of John Locke*, ed. J. L. Axtell (Cambridge: Cambridge University Press, 1960), §81.

26. Ibid., chap. 6, §55.

27. Rousseau, preface to *Emile*, 2.

28. James Dwyer develops this critical argument in his "Changing the Conversation."

29. Arneil, "Becoming versus Being," in Archard and Macleod, *Moral and Political Status of Children*, 72.

30. Anthony Cunningham, "Kantian Ethics and Intimate Attachments," *American Philosophical Quarterly* 36, no. 4 (1999): 279–94.

31. See Tamar Schapiro, "What Is a Child?" *Ethics* 109 (July 1999): 715–38.

32. Jean Piaget, *The Origins of Intelligence in Children* (New York: International University Press, 1952); Lawrence Kohlberg, *The Philosophy of Moral Development* (San Francisco: Harper and Row, 1981).

33. Schapiro, "What Is a Child?" 716.

34. Arneil, "Becoming versus Being," in Archard and Macleod, *Moral and Political Status of Children*. Arneil advocates an ethics of care as a substitute for a conceptualization of "becoming" that characterizes rights-based liberal theories.

35. More on school choice in chapter 6.

36. Alma Gottlieb, "Where Have All the Babies Gone? Toward an Anthropology of Infants (and Their Caretakers)," *Anthropological Quarterly* 73, no. 3 (2000): 121–32.

37. One notable exception is Agnieszka Jaworska, "Caring and Internality," *Philosophy and Phenomenological Research* 74, no. 3 (2007): 529–68.

38. Grace Clement, *Care, Autonomy, and Justice: Feminism and the Ethic of Care* (Boulder, CO: Westview Press, 1996).

39. Critical discussions of this view are offered in Jean B. Elshtain, *Public Man, Private Woman: Women in Social and Political Thought* (Princeton, NJ: Princeton University Press, 1981); Nancy J. Hirschman and Christine Di Stephano, eds., *Revisioning the Political: Feminist Reconstructions of Traditional Concepts in Western Political Theory* (Boulder, CO: Westview Press, 1996); Nancy Chodorow, *The Reproduction of Mothering: Psychoanalysis and the Sociology of Gender* (Berkeley: University of California Press, 1978); Edith Kurzweil, *Freudians and Feminists* (Boulder, CO: Westview Press, 1995).

40. Schapiro, "What Is a Child?" 715.

41. See a related and engaging debate of the demands of civic education from children and from immigrants, and how they relate to children's rights and moral status in society, in Joe Coleman, "Answering Susan: Liberalism, Civic Education, and the Status of Younger Persons," in Archard and Macleod, *Moral and Political Status of Children*, 160–82.

42. Schapiro, "What Is a Child?" 717.

43. Tolerating children's socially objectionable ways of expression is justified for other reasons beyond understanding their unfamiliarity with social norms. See Joan F. Goodman, "Niceness and the Limits of Rules," *Journal of Moral Education* 30, no. 4 (December 2001): 349–60.

44. Purdy, *In Their Best Interest?*; Cunningham, *Kantian Ethics*.

45. Amy Gutmann, *Identity in Democracy* (Princeton, NJ: Princeton University Press, 2003), 69–73.

46. Maria Montessori, *The Discovery of the Child* (Madras, India: Kalakshetra Publications, 1966); Dwyer, "Changing the Conversation," as well as his *Vouchers Within Reason: A Child-Centered Approach to Education Reform* (Ithaca, NY: Cornell University Press, 2002).

Chapter 5
Exit with Caution: On Culture and Choice

1. Susan Moller Okin, "Mistresses of Their Own Destiny: Group Rights, Gender, and Realistic Rights of Exit," *Ethics* 112 (January 2002): 205–30, at 205–6.

2. This line of argument aligns with David Plotke's recent account of political incorporation as a preferable response to anti-democratic political communities in a democracy over toleration and repression. There are some differences in our views, which I do not explore here; generally,

Plotke focuses on political responses while here I put more emphasis on social structure. See David Plotke, "Democratic Polities and Anti-democratic Politics," *Theoria* 53, no. 111 (December 2006): 6–44.

3. Bhikhu Parekh, *Rethinking Multiculturalism: Cultural Diversity and Political Theory* (Cambridge, MA: Harvard University Press, 2006), 143.

4. Colin McLeod, "Shaping Children's Convictions," *Theory and Research in Education* 1, no. 3 (2003): 315–30; in *Surviving Diversity*, Jeff Spinner-Halev argues for liberal accommodation of restrictive communities: Jeff Spinner-Halev, *Surviving Diversity: Religion and Democratic Citizenship* (Baltimore: Johns Hopkins University Press, 2000); in *Multicultural Jurisdictions: Cultural Differences and Women's Rights* (Cambridge: Cambridge University Press, 2001), Ayelet Shachar calls for tolerance and respect for deep cultural disagreements, which still requires exit rights; Stephen Macedo, in *Diversity and Distrust: Civic Education in a Multicultural Democracy* (Cambridge, MA: Harvard University Press, 2000), makes the case for intervening in restrictive communities to support the main values of the liberal democracy within which they live; see a discussion of some of these views in Avigail Eisenberg, "Diversity and Equality: Three Approaches to Cultural and Sexual Difference," *Journal of Political Philosophy* 11, no. 1 (March 2003): 41–64.

5. William Galston, "Two Concepts of Liberalism," *Ethics* 105, no. 3 (1995): 516–34, at 523.

6. Harry Brighouse, "Civic Education and Liberal Legitimacy," *Ethics* 108 (July 1998): 719–45; Eamonn Callan, *Creating Citizens* (Oxford: Clarendon Press, 1997); Amy Gutmann, *Democratic Education* (Princeton, NJ: Princeton University Press, 1999); Macedo, *Diversity and Distrust*; Rob Reich, *Bridging Liberalism and Multiculturalism in Education* (Chicago: University of Chicago Press, 2002).

7. William Galston, *Liberal Pluralism: The Implications of Value Pluralism for Political Theory and Practice* (Cambridge: Cambridge University Press, 2002); Spinner-Halev, *Surviving Diversity*; Shelly Burtt, "Religious Parents, Secular Schools: A Liberal Defense of an Illiberal Education," *Review of Politics* 56, no. 1 (Winter 1994): 51–70; Chandran Kukathas, "Are There Any Cultural Rights?" *Political Theory* 20, no. 1 (1992): 105–39; Frances Kroeker and Stephen Norris, "An Unwarranted Fear of Religious Schooling," *Canadian Journal of Education* 30, no. 1 (2007): 269–90.

8. K. Anthony Appiah, "Identity, Authenticity, Survival: Multicultural Societies and Social Reproduction," in *Multiculturalism: Examining the Politics of Recognition*, ed. Amy Gutmann (Princeton, NJ: Princeton University Press, 1994), 155.

9. Okin, "Mistresses of Their Own Destiny"; Will Kymlicka, *Multicul-*

tural Citizenship: A Liberal Theory of Minority Rights (Oxford: Oxford University Press, 1995); Galston, *Liberal Pluralism*; Chandran Kukathas, "Liberalism and Multiculturalism: The Politics of Indifference," *Political Theory* 26, no. 5 (1998): 686–99.

10. Jacob Levy, *The Multiculturalism of Fear* (New York: Oxford University Press, 2000), 112.

11. Susan Moller Okin, *Is Multiculturalism Bad for Women?* (Princeton, NJ: Princeton University Press, 1999), 9. Another example is the case of Julia Martinez and the Pueblo policy of disenfranchising women who marry out, as discussed in Amy Gutmann's *Identity in Democracy* (Princeton, NJ: Princeton University Press, 2003).

12. Kwame Anthony Appiah, *The Ethics of Identity* (Princeton, NJ: Princeton University Press 2005), 77. Appiah goes on to investigate the weaknesses and strengths of exit rights as a mechanism for protecting individuals. Loyal to his commitment to individual autonomy understood through a complex lens of personal and social psychology, he asserts that it is possible to maintain state neutrality in the treatment of different groups by treating "people of diverse social identities with equal respect" (91).

13. See Avigail Eisenberg and Jeff Spinner-Halev, eds., *Minorities Within Minorities* (Cambridge: Cambridge University Press, 2005).

14. See Kymlicka, *Multicultural Citizenship*, 80–84, for an elaboration of the idea of living a life from the inside. See also the discussion in Brighouse, "Civic Education and Liberal Legitimacy," 730–31.

15. The comparison of exit to divorce is only partial: individuals usually enter marriage as adults, and other distinctions—related, for example, to the acquisition of property—give rise to the regulation of property division following a divorce. Similarly, child support is regulated as a way to protect children from some of the adverse consequences of divorce. Leaving a culture to which one was born is closer to the decision to leave one's home and family of origin, a decision that is entirely unregulated.

16. I am leaving aside here the possibility of immigration as a form of exit because it offers very different horizons and creates different practical and ethical challenges to the exiting individual. See Eamonn Callan, "The Ethics of Assimilation," *Ethics* (April 2005): 471–500.

17. Ayelet Shachar, *Multicultural Jurisdictions: Cultural Differences and Women's Rights* (Cambridge: Cambridge University Press, 2001), 43–44.

18. *Wisconsin v. Yoder*, 406 U.S. 205 (1972), which provided exemption for Amish children in Wisconsin from the final two years of compulsory education and allowed them to leave after the eighth grade; *Mozert v. Hawkins County Board of Education*, 827 F.2d 1058 1987 U.S. App, in

which a group of fundamentalist parents did not receive the exemption they requested from a curriculum they found offensive.

19. *Santa Clara Pueblo v. Martinez*, 436 U.S. 49 (1978). See the discussion on the identity aspects of this case in Amy Gutmann, *Identity in Democracy* (Princeton, NJ: Princeton University Press, 2002), 45–46.

20. Spinner-Halev, *Surviving Diversity*, 77.

21. John Tomasi, *Liberalism beyond Justice* (Princeton, NJ: Princeton University Press, 2001).

22. Bruce Ackerman, *Social Justice in the Liberal State* (New Haven, CT: Yale University Press, 1981); Callan, *Creating Citizens*; Brighouse, "Civic Education and Liberal Legitimacy."

23. Michael Hand, "Against Autonomy as an Educational Aim," *Oxford Review of Education* 32, no. 4 (September 2006): 535–50.

24. Burtt, "Religious Parents, Secular Schools," at 64.

25. Ibid., 65.

26. Ibid., 67.

27. See Reich, *Bridging Liberalism and Multiculturalism in Education*, chap. 4.

28. Brighouse, "Civic Education and Liberal Legitimacy."

29. Emile Lester, "The Right to Reasonable Exit and Education for Moderate Autonomy," *Review of Politics* 68 (2006): 612–35, at 614.

30. Galston, "Two Concepts of Liberalism," at 523.

31. Galston, *Liberal Pluralism: The Implications of Value Pluralism for Political Theory and Practice*, at 28.

32. William A. Galston, *The Practice of Liberal Pluralism* (Cambridge: Cambridge University Press, 2005), 41.

33. Spinner-Halev, *Surviving Diversity*, 70.

34. Ibid., 71.

35. Ibid., 72.

36. This is based on a Pew survey, February 2008. The data are available at http://religions.pewforum.org/ (accessed February 26, 2008). I have no data as to how many of these "switchers" were originally members of non-reflective or encompassing communities, and clearly the very description of a group as such is often controversial. What these numbers are meant to illustrate is mostly the wide availability of knowledge about "other options" despite the fact that autonomy is not being formally taught in public schools, and that many religious families refrain from sending their children to these schools.

37. This figure takes into account movement between Protestant denominations.

38. Certain subcultures do give some room for discussion of exit, as with the much-discussed Amish practice of sending youth for a year "outside." There is some debate about the prevalence of this practice. In any case, it does not correlate well with the idea of exit rights, as it is a onetime opportunity, and those who choose to stay close the door behind them, ideally (from the Amish perspective) for good. Many other comprehensive cultures discourage exit altogether.

Chapter 6
School Choice as a Bounded Ideal

1. For supporters of school choice as a free market tool to increase quality, see John E. Chubb and Terry M. Moe, *Politics, Markets, and America's Schools* (Washington, DC: Brookings Institute, 1990); and Joseph P. Viteretti, *Choosing Equality: School Choice, the Constitution and Civil Society* (Washington, DC: Brookings Institute, 1999). Some liberal supporters of school choice as reflecting liberal-democratic values are Amy Gutmann, *Democratic Education* (Princeton, NJ: Princeton University Press, 1999); and Meira Levinson, *The Demands of Liberal Education* (New York: Oxford University Press, 1999). Egalitarian supporters of school choice programs as potentially contributing to social justice are Harry Brighouse, *School Choice and Social Justice* (New York: Oxford University Press, 2000); and Adam Swift, *How Not to Be a Hypocrite* (London: Routledge, 2003).

2. Amy Gutmann, *Democratic Education*; Stephen Gilles, "On Educating Children: A Parentalist Manifesto," *University of Chicago Law Review* 63 (1997): 937–99; James G. Dwyer, "Changing the Conversation about Children's Education," in *Moral and Political Education,* ed. Stephen Macedo and Yael Tamir (New York: New York University Press, 2002), 314–58.

3. I begin with assuming that school choice in some form is part of the existing policies; I therefore do not debate its relative merits as compared to no-choice policies.

4. Mark Schneider, Paul Teske, Christine Roch, and Melissa Marshal, "Networks to Nowhere: Segregation and Stratification in Networks of Information about Schools," *American Journal of Political Science* 41, no. 4 (October 1997): 1201–23, at 1202. As discussed later, Schneider et al. criticize this assumption.

5. From a speech by Education Secretary Rodney Paige at the Heritage

Foundation, upon the introduction of school choice to Washington DC students, January 28, 2004, http://www.dcpswatch.com/vouchers/040128. htm (accessed November 15, 2007).

6. Immanuel Kant, *Conflict of the Faculties*, trans. Mary J. Gregor (Lincoln: University of Nebraska Press, 1992), 43.

7. Stephen J. Ball, *Class Strategies and the Education Market: The Middle Classes and Social Advantage* (New York: RoutledgeFalmer, 2003), at 111.

8. Keith Dowding, "Choice: Its Increase and Its Value," *British Journal of Political Science* 22, no. 3 (July 1992), 301–14, at 313.

9. Daniel Kahneman, "Maps of Bounded Rationality: Psychology for Behavioral Economics," *American Economic Review* 93, no. 5 (December 2003): 1449–75, at 1449.

10. See, for example, Edward A. Zelinsky, "Do Tax Expenditures Create Framing Effects? Volunteer Firefighters, Property Tax Exemptions, and the Paradox of Tax Expenditure Analysis," *Virginia Tax Review* 24 (2005).

11. Sheena S. Iyengar and Mark R. Lepper, "When Choice Is Demotivating: Can One Desire Too Much of a Good Thing?" *Journal of Personality and Social Psychology* 79, no. 6 (December 2000): 995–1006.

12. Sheena S. Iyengar, Gur Huberman, and Wei Jiang, "How Much Choice Is Too Much? Contributions to 401(k) Retirement Plans," in *Pension Design and Structure: New Lessons from Behavioral Finance*, ed. Olivia S. Mitchell and Stephen P. Utkus (Oxford: Oxford University Press, 2004), 83–95. In marketing, see the unique but important Marianne Mullainathan Bertrand and Eldar Sendhil Shafir, "Behavioral Economics and Marketing in Aid of Decision-Making Among the Poor," *Journal of Public Policy and Marketing* 25, no. 1 (Spring 2006): 8–23.

13. Yaniv Hanoch and Thomas Rice, "Can Limiting Choice Increase Social Welfare? The Elderly and Health Insurance," *Milbank Quarterly* 84, no. 1 (2006): 37–73.

14. Classic examples are Robert Entman, *Projections of Power: Framing News, Public Opinion, and U.S. Foreign Policy* (Chicago: University of Chicago Press 2003); and Pipa Norris, *Framing Terrorism: The News Media, the Government and the Public* (London: Routledge, 2003). Thus, in communication research, the study of political news is usually not studied as a direct tool for informing citizens about current events, but rather in terms of framing theory and the citizens' constructed heuristics of judgment.

15. Colin Camerer, "Wanting, Liking, and Learning: Neuroscience and Paternalism," *University of Chicago Law Review* 73 (Winter 2006): 87–110.

16. One important study that was partially inspired by this literature is

Mark Schneider, Paul Teske, and Melissa Marshall, *Choosing Schools: Consumer Choice and the Quality of American Schools* (Princeton, NJ: Princeton University Press, 2000).

17. Various studies examined the effect of school choice. See John F. Witte, "School Choice and Student Performance," in *Holding Schools Accountable: Performance-Based Reform in Education*, ed. Helen F. Ladd (Washington, DC: Brookings Institute, 1996). This study found no relative achievement gains to choice students. Another study found significant gains in both math and reading; see Jay P. Greene, Paul E. Peterson, and Jiangtao Du, "The Effectiveness of School Choice: The Milwaukee Experiment" (Occasional Paper no. 97-1, Harvard University Education Policy and Governance, March 1997).

18. U.S. Department of Education, "State and Local Implementation of the No Child Left Behind Act," vols. III–IV, http://www.ed.gov/rschstat/ eval/disadv/nclb-accountability/index.html (accessed January 15, 2009).

19. In 2007, 15 percent of the schools in Houston Independent School District were deemed "failing," making about 17,500 students eligible for transfer. Few of their families took advantage of this opportunity, primarily because the official approval for transfer was provided on October 8, six weeks after the start of the school year. "Delay Leaves Students Who Want to Transfer in Limbo," *Houston Chronicle*, August 14, 2008, A1, http:// www.chron.com/ (accessed September 21, 2008).

20. William Samuelson and Richard Zeckhauser, "Status Quo Bias in Decision-Making," *Journal of Risk and Uncertainty* 1, no. 1 (March 1988): 7–59.

21. M. E. Graue, J. Kroeger, and D. Prager, "A Bakhtinian Analysis of Particular Home-School Relations," *American Educational Research Journal* 38, no. 3 (2001): 467–98, at 471.

22. Ball, *Class Strategies*, 151.

23. In a study evaluating the first year of implementing the Washington DC opportunity scholarships, 74 percent of scholarship (or choice) parents assigned their children's school a grade of A or B, compared to 55 percent of the control group. Patrick J. Wolf, *Evaluation of the DC Opportunity Scholarship Fund after One Year* (Washington, DC: Institute of Education Sciences, U.S. Department of Education, June 2007), 56.

24. Stephen Gorard, *School Choice and the Established Market* (Aldershot: Ashgate, 1997).

25. Ball, *Class Strategies*, 102.

26. Meira Levinson, *The Demands of Liberal Education* (Oxford: Oxford University Press, 2002), 155.

27. Lois André-Bechely, "Public School Choice at the Intersection of Voluntary Integration and Not-So-Good Neighborhood Schools: Lessons from Parents' Experiences," *Educational Administration Quarterly* 41, no. 2 (April 2005): 267–305, at 271.

28. Ibid., 287.

29. Ibid., 280.

30. Ibid., 291.

31. Courtney A. Bell, "Real Options: The Role of Choice Sets in the Selection of Schools," *Teachers College Record*, January 9, 2006, http://www.tcrecord.org, ID no. 12277 (accessed September 25, 2009).

32. Amy Stuart Wells, "African-American Students' View of School Choice," in *Who Chooses? Who Loses? Culture, Institutions and the Unequal Effects of School Choice*, ed. Bruce F. Fuller and Richard Elmore (New York: Teachers College Press, 1996), 25–49.

33. M. Schneider, P. Teske, C. Roch, and M. Marschall, "Networks to Nowhere: Segregation and Stratification in Networks of Information about Schools," *American Journal of Political Science* 41 (1997): 1201–23, at 1201.

34. For more on the accessibility of schools to higher SES parents, see Daniel J. McGrath and Peter J. Kuriloff, "'They're Going to Tear the Doors Off This Place': Upper-Middle-Class Parent School Involvement and the Educational Opportunities of Other People's Children," *Educational Policy* 13 (1999): 603–29.

35. Thomas Stewart, Patrick J. Wolf, and Stephen Q. Cornman, "Parent and Student Voices on the First Year of the DC Opportunity Scholarship Program," *Peabody Journal of Education* 82, no. 2 (2007): 311–86.

36. Most scholars on the topic, including those who are committed to the logic of the market, acknowledge the need to regulate the provision of schooling. An exception is James Tooley, who is more concerned with the provision side, and focused on the need to create a real market by eliminating public provision. See James Tooley, *Reclaiming Education* (London: Continuum, 2000). Scholars who favor regulation often attempt to increase cost effectiveness or achieve specific social outcomes and not, as the current argument goes, to respond to the needs of the choosing agents or to promote egalitarian goals.

37. Harry Brighouse, *School Choice and Social Justice* (Oxford: Oxford University Press, 2000), 194.

38. Herbert Gintis, "Political Economy of School Choice," *Teachers College Record* 96, no. 3 (Spring 1995): 492–511.

39. Choice within schools is as important as choice across or among schools, as location is a decisive factor for many parents, particularly as

young children are involved. Proximity plays less of a decisive role in high school choice, as indicated in Valerie E. Lee, Robert G. Croninger, and Julia B. Smith, "Equity and Choice in Detroit," in Fuller and Elmore, *Who Chooses? Who Loses?* 70–91.

Conclusion
Structured Paternalism and the Landscape of Choice

1. See, for example, Leonard Beeghley, *The Structure of Social Stratification in the United States* (New York: Pearson, 2004).

INDEX